The Therapy Crouch

EBURY
SPOTLIGHT

1

Ebury Spotlight, an imprint of Ebury Publishing
20 Vauxhall Bridge Road
London SW1V 2SA

Ebury Spotlight is part of the Penguin Random House group
of companies whose addresses can be found at global.
penguinrandomhouse.com

Penguin
Random House
UK

First published by Ebury Spotlight in 2023
This edition was published in 2024

www.penguin.co.uk

A CIP catalogue record for this book is available from the British
Library

ISBN 9781529918021

Printed and bound in Great Britain by Clays Ltd, Elcograf S.p.A.

The authorised representative in the EEA is Penguin Random House
Ireland, Morrison Chambers, 32 Nassau Street, Dublin D02 YH68

Penguin Random House is committed to a sustainable future for our
business, our readers and our planet. This book is made from Forest
Stewardship Council® certified paper.

FSC www.fsc.org MIX Paper | Supporting responsible forestry FSC® C018179

The Therapy Crouch

In Search of Never a Happy ~~Ever~~ After

PETER CROUCH & ABBEY CLANCY

There's no better story than a love story.

Abbey: For my husband Peeeete! You are my world, I love you.

Peter: For my wife Abbey, you're simply the best.

Contents

Introduction

One minute you are checking each other out online or in a pub, the next you are exchanging numbers, going on dates and getting serious. First dates, first times and first fights all come and go. You meet each other's friends and family, go on holiday, make plans for a future together. If things go really well there's a proposal, diamond rings, wedding dresses and first dances to pick, honeymoons to plan, lives to live together. You settle down, make a home and start a family, and before you know it, you've gone from a chance meeting by the loos in the Mosquito nightclub in Liverpool, to looking around and finding the two of you have become a family of six. Well, maybe that's our story, but dating, relationships and falling in love are a roller coaster ride that we all get to go on at some point.

Relationships can be happy – being with your other person can feel like home – but partners can wind you up and drive you mad too, so we're here to talk about it all: the good, the bad *and* the ugly. We'll share our highs and our lows, and the day-to-day mundane bits in between too, as well as what works and doesn't work for us.

This is absolutely, definitely *not* a self-help book; it does contain some 'advice', but it's the kind of advice in inverted commas that you definitely should be wary of living your life by.

So come on in and join us as we embark on an A to Z journey to find that elusive happy ever after.

A

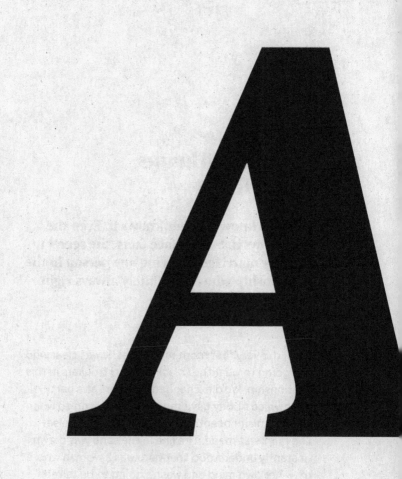

A is for *Absolutely Always Being Right*

The kids know it. Peter knows it. Even the dog knows it. So let's face facts: the secret to a happy marriage is having one person in the relationship who is absolutely always right.

Peter: And that person ain't me.

From the very first moment we met, it was clear who was going to wear the (black leather) trousers in this relationship. We'd exchanged numbers at a party, after which Abbey gave me a proper talking-to when she saw me innocently chatting to someone else. The mark was made. The line in the sand was drawn. I instantly understood that here was a woman who knew her own mind and wasn't going to be talked out of it.

And I respect her for that. When she says – as she frequently does – 'I'm always right', I nod and agree. It's normally true and life's easier that way. Even when it *isn't* true, which happens perhaps once every seven or eight years, I just nod and go along with it. I like a quiet life.

Abbey: I have a very clear idea of how I want things to work. I like the house to look good, I like the kids to behave and do their homework, and I like us to be on time for things. It's a lot to think about when you have four children and a busy life, so things need to run to order. That's only going to happen if Pete bows to the inevitable truth that I know what I'm talking about, far more than he does.

Absolutely always being right can be a strain, though. Sometimes it's good to have a wingman who doesn't always see being right as a priority. That's where Pete comes in. If I get frustrated that something isn't quite going to plan, it can be comforting to hear him say, 'OK, so we forgot a bag, we're still alive, that's all that matters ...' Even then, though, I can't help feeling that if everything had just been done the way I wanted from the very beginning, we'd never be in this situation.

Peter: Long story short: if everyone does what Abbey says, it's best all round.

Abbey: It makes life a lot less complicated if the pecking order is clear. In this household, I'm in charge.

Peter: Happily, though, I'm not quite at the bottom of the pecking order. The dog always – *always* – listens to me. He's the only one in the house that does, and I love him for that.

A is for irport Abs

There's Abs. Calm, patient, fun-loving Abs. And then there's Airport Abs.

A very different beast altogether ...

Peter: Airport Abs emerges early from her lair the morning of departure for our holiday. She has high hopes for the day to come, as she has been meticulously planning it for weeks, if not months (see P is for Packing and Planning). The suitcases are organised with the military precision of a regimental sergeant major. The taxi to the airport is booked with ample time to spare, just in case there's a traffic jam or a major natural disaster on the M25. The passports and tickets are neatly arranged. Everything is planned down to the last detail.

But here's the problem. There is no Plan B. So if Plan A fails us, we're buggered.

Which is why, while Airport Abs is charging round the house getting ready for the off, my priority is to gather the children around me, to get down on my knees and ask them – no, *beg* them – to be good.

'Don't do anything to wind your mum up,' I'll say. 'Because, kids, trust me on this, none of us wants that ...'

Abbey: I like – I *need* – to be at the airport nice and early because travelling with four kids (five, if you include Peter) is no picnic. It's a logistical nightmare. We are, happily, over the stage of having to carry formula milk, which practically required a suitcase of its own and always managed to leak into the bottom of my hand luggage – not a smell you want to be faced with every time you root around for a snack or a toy. But even now I'll be running around the house making last-minute collections of Calpol, plasters, bite cream, stuff to keep the kids entertained, snacks for the plane, extra snacks to replace the snacks that I know they'll already have eaten by the time we get to the airport ... The list is endless, and I feel the first stirrings of rage when I see the rest of the family dilly-dallying around with no particular sense of urgency. Don't they know what's at stake here?

Pete has two jobs on airport days: putting out the cat litter and shutting the windows – but you can be sure that by the time the taxi draws up outside the house (late, inevitably) the litter will remain untouched, the windows will be wide open. So I'll take on the role of cat lady and window woman too.

We'll pile our six suitcases, four rucksacks and two pushchairs into the back of the taxi. I like us to be organised – neat, tidy and clean – but by the time we reach the airport the kids will be covered in chewing gum, smeared with snacks; they'll have rooted through my bags, getting stuff out, losing it, using it, not putting it back ... I'd be in a better position to stop them if I wasn't so focused on the taxi and how my Plan A already seems to have gone to the wall. *Why is it late? Why's he driving this way? Surely the other way is quicker. We're going to miss the plane ...*

I have a confession to make, which is that I don't much like flying. So rather than admit that I'm scared, I try to control everything around me. I can't help myself. I want so much control that I *lose* control. By the time we stagger out of the taxi, we don't look like the perfect, cool, debonair family I imagine us to be. We look like *The Beverly Hillbillies*. And we haven't even entered the terminal yet.

Peter: Ah, the terminal. I have a very distinct strategy once we get inside. It is a sausage-based strategy. Abbey is especially fond of the sausages served in the airport lounge. Each to their own. If I can keep her focused on the lounge sausages, my hope is that Airport Abs will retreat somewhat, and our passage through check-in, bag drop and security will be more relaxed for everyone involved, including her.

One holiday, I couldn't remember the membership numbers for the lounge. My ineptitude was about as well received as you might imagine. Airport Abs was denied her lounge sausages and consigned to a three-hour stint in a Gatwick burger joint. We don't mention this traumatic event anymore. It is a moment best forgotten.

Abbey: It's well known that travel food has no calories. You can eat as many sausages as you like at the airport, guilt-free. Whole bag of fizzy jellies? No problem! Doritos are like air if you're sitting on a train. So it's true that lounge sausages are an effective incentive. But still: the moment I set foot inside the terminal, the anxiety builds. The kids are always pretty well behaved, but they're excited about going on holiday and are full of energy, so they indulge in their fair share of swinging off the queue barriers, pushing each other around on trolleys and generally adding to the mayhem and to my blood pressure. We're fairly recognisable as a family, so I'm desperate not to draw any more attention to ourselves than we need to. Which is more easily said than done. You can't imagine how much I'm sweating as we try to keep all our belongings - and children - together. As I try to organise six passports, six boarding passes and six people and not lose anything or anyone, chaos descends. I try to keep Airport Abs in her box, but it's no good. I feel like I need to have my eyes on all four of the kids all the time. What if I lose them? What if they're kidnapped? How do I deal with one of them needing the toilet while the other is hiding behind the trollies? It's manic ... I'm stressed ... the red mist descends ...

Peter: Which makes the acquisition of lounge sausages all the more urgent. So I manoeuvre the family into the lounge as quickly as possible and I load up Abbey's plate ...

It's only once we've boarded the plane, settled into our seats and taken off that I can finally feel able to sit back, relax and have a drink. It's a celebration that we've finally dealt with the stress of Airport Abs and we're going on holiday.

Abbey: Peter has a drink? I wouldn't know. We're normally separated by a line of children. We gave up sitting next to each other on a plane years ago, so I've no idea what he gets up to on a flight. All I know is this: I still can't fully relax because there's another airport to be negotiated at the other end. More queues ... more delays ... more passport officials ... more stress ...

Peter: I'm quite Zen about it all by this time.

Abbey: And I now know that's because you've spent your flight necking gin and tonics from the trolley ...

A is for Animals

For a man who was never all that into children or animals when Abbey first met him, Peter certainly now has his fair share of both ...

Peter: Our house is like a zoo. In fact, it's worse than a zoo. A zoo has strange animals and exhibits. Each animal has its own enclosure. There is order and calm. Our house is more like a city farm. It's bursting with animals and children. There are simply too many breathing things to worry about. As if four kids aren't enough to keep us busy, Abbey has embraced and taken in half the animal kingdom, and she shows no signs of stopping ...

Abbey: I didn't have pets growing up, so now that I'm an adult I'm living out my childhood dream. When Pete asked me to move in, I came with all my stuff and two tiny little kittens in a box. I think it's brilliant for kids to grow up in the company of animals – it teaches them so much. Although I will admit that the trauma of losing a pet can be difficult for them. When Sophia was four she had a hamster called Katie, a sweet, fluffy little thing that she completely doted on. She would play with Katie before school, when she got home – she would play with Katie every waking hour ...

And then, one morning, Katie wouldn't wake up.

I was nine months pregnant and had been up all night vomiting with terrible food poisoning. I came down to a scene of absolute bedlam. Sophia was wailing, 'Katie, wake up! I love you!' Peter had tears streaming down his face and was trying to give that tiny hamster mouth-to-mouth resuscitation.

Peter: I tried to perform CPR. It was a Russian dwarf hamster, tiny enough to fit in the palm of my hand. I pumped away with my thumb, but eventually I came to the realisation that there was nothing more I could do. Katie had passed on to the great hamster wheel in the sky. I took her to the vet and pretended to Sophia that they could make sure Katie went to hamster heaven. As I was driving there, it occurred to me that I could swap her for a new hamster and say that she'd been resurrected like Jesus. Hallelujah! But it proved impossible to get a like-for-like replacement, so my plans to enact a miracle were scuppered and we had to buckle up and bear it.

You'd have thought that a traumatic experience would put us off the whole animal thing. Think again.

Abbey: Animals have just always been part of our married life. Pete bought me a horse once. I used to ride it every day, even Christmas Day. And early on in our relationship we got our cats. We had two fur babies and felt like a little family. Pete was far more accepting of pets in those days, but I suspect it was because he was trying to impress me. His attitude has changed somewhat of late, and he seems strangely resistant to the addition of any new creatures. So when, during lockdown, I decided it would be lovely for the family to have a new puppy to train and walk, I had to be sneaky. I had to put on my thinking cap. Maybe I could overcome his reluctance if I found us the same breed of puppy that he grew up with? Surely a lovely little Labrador would transport him back to happy memories of his carefree childhood!

He succumbed, and that little Labrador became our miracle pet. He was ill as a puppy. He couldn't walk and we had to feed him with a syringe every hour.

Peter: We'd finally got to a point where our children didn't need night feeds, and here we were, awake every hour of the night, doing it all over again, but for a dog. A dog! It's absolutely mental.

Abbey: Unfortunately, I forgot that Labs eat absolutely everything in sight and shed black hairs all over the place. Obviously he's gorgeous and I adore him, but if I hadn't been forced into subterfuge, I might have chosen a non-moulting labradoodle. Perhaps that could be our next pet ...

Peter: No more! One family can only cope with a certain number of sentient beings. We've got two cats and a dog, and sometimes we'll have family visiting and they'll bring their dogs too. Great Danes chasing in and out of the house. Mess everywhere. Total. Chaos. But Abbey wants more. She wants mini-donkeys in the garden.

Abbey: Not just the garden! I'd have them walking into the kitchen taking a carrot from the worktop. I would literally die for that.

Peter: You would literally be over it as soon as it had happened once. The novelty would never last, and it would be me who ended up having to look after them, even though I never wanted them in the first place. And my enthusiasm for clearing up donkey dung is limited.

But Abbey would totally get some donkeys if I didn't put my foot down, and I'm not even certain they would be the strangest beasts in our menagerie. At Easter, we hatch our own ducks. We put the eggs in the incubator, and the ducklings hatch for Easter Sunday. The kids love it. I find myself sitting on the couch with a duck next to me for company, thinking, *How did* this *happen?*

And once, I called Abbey when she was in the car with the kids. We chatted for a while and I suddenly heard a noise that sounded suspiciously like, 'Baaaaaa ...'

'What's that?' I said.

'Nothing,' Abbey replied, all innocence.

But it wasn't nothing. It was very far from being nothing. I came home to find two orphaned lambs in the sitting room.

Abbey: I'd just been to get them from the farm when Peter called. He says he hates all the animals, but I think he protests too much. I've come home to find them all wrapped up in a towel, being fed from a bottle, with Pete filming them. And for me, it's all about making the kids happy. Surely it's better to be in the garden hand-rearing a baby lamb than playing *Roblox* in a darkened room for hours. Surely the best birthday present ever is to wake up and find a little puppy that is completely yours. I can't think of anything better.

So watch this space. Our menagerie is far from complete.

B

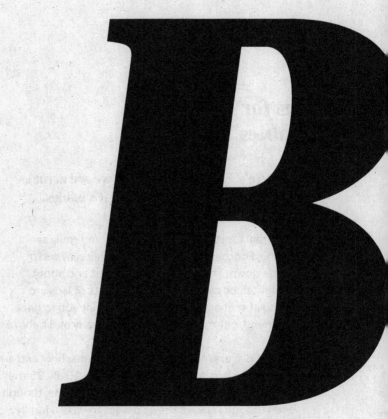

B is for abies

If there's a subject on which we are actual, real-life, bona-fide experts ... it's babies.

Peter: It's a real footballer thing, having your family so young. Football clubs encourage their players to settle down. They don't want you out and about in nightclubs causing trouble, like lots of lads are doing at that age. They genuinely want you to get a girlfriend, get married, settle down early and behave.

Lots of players meet their girlfriends at school and are expecting children by the time they're 20. By 25 they have three kids and a quiet family life. For me, though, even though I always knew I'd want to have a family eventually, babies weren't on my radar for a long time. Women tend to think more about that kind of thing. Abbey certainly did.

Abbey: I'm 12 years older than my youngest brother and sister, so I was almost a second mum to them. The maternal instinct was always there, so I really wanted to have a baby. Looking back, I wonder what we were thinking, trying for a baby when I was only in my early twenties. But we ended up trying for a long time. It took me two and a half years to get pregnant at first. And to start with, we were pretty relaxed about the whole business. We certainly didn't give a thought to anything so unromantic as ovulation timing. Eventually, though, I was taking my temperature every day and shouting, 'Pete, come on! It's now! *Right now! Get your kit off!*' For him, the novelty wore off pretty quickly. By the end he was complaining, 'I feel used. You're just using me for my sperm.'

Peter: I've got feelings too, you know. I'm sure there are plenty of men out there who'd love to have been in my shoes, but it felt like a transaction. I felt like a tool (insert your own joke here).

Abbey: As falling pregnant was so much harder than we expected, finally getting that positive pregnancy test result was the best feeling in the world. I was so grateful and excited, but at the same time I felt a massive pressure to grow our longed-for little baby in the right way.

Peter: Abbey was amazing. She never put a foot wrong the whole way through the pregnancy.

Abbey: I didn't drink, and I was super-careful with everything I ate – no goat's cheese or brie for me, which, I have to tell you, was a sacrifice. I wouldn't change the cat litter. I wouldn't use oven cleaner (less of a sacrifice). I stuck by all the rules. I wanted everything to be perfect, and it was. When Sophia was born she was like a little rosebud, so delicate and perfect, the most beautiful baby. We were so proud bringing her home from hospital in her little car seat. The house felt so calm. So lovely. Just us.

Peter: It was such a wonderful feeling leaving the house as a couple and coming home as a family of three. We were instantly bonded for ever.

Abbey: From the moment we first saw Sophia, Pete has always been the most amazing dad. He can't do enough for his family. He's loving, patient and kind, and I adore seeing him with them.

And after our slow start, we ended up being pretty prolific in the baby department. By the end of our baby-making odyssey, Pete barely had to look at me for me to fall pregnant. Our families would roll their eyes and say, 'Not again!'

However …

I adore babies, and it took so much for us to get pregnant in the first place that I sometimes feel bad for complaining about pregnancy at all, but here goes. When I hear women say how much they loved being pregnant, I just can't relate to it in any way. I was so ill with my last two pregnancies that I could barely lift a finger. I vomited all day. My hair fell out. I was covered in rashes. I had piles, cystitis, thrush – I had the lot. I couldn't smell anything, couldn't eat anything. It was like being car sick every day for nine months.

Now, if the roles were reversed, I'm pretty sure I'd be an attentive nurse. I'd be checking in on my suffering patient, bringing them cups of tea, preparing them lovely little snacks, keeping them company. Pete's idea of looking after me was not quite that: 'Oh, you stay in bed, love.' Door shut, no contact for the next 12 hours! I would lie there, not only feeling dreadful but also bored out of my mind ...

Peter: Trouble is that Pregnancy Abs is very similar to Airport Abs, only a lot more hormonal. I knew that if I ventured into the bedroom, I'd get shouted out. It was like dealing with a banshee, only less reasonable. Everyone was scared of her. The only way I could deal with it was to provide regular trays of food and water, like she was a prisoner and I was pushing her rations through the hatch in the cell door. In fact, Abbey being pregnant always reminds me of the scene in *The Green Mile* when John Coffey removes the sadness and blows out the demons. The minute she gives birth, all the badness goes away and she becomes Abbey again. It's always quite nice to have her back, actually.

Abbey: Growing a baby inside you is such a huge honour and a miracle, but everything else that comes along with it is just horrific. I've often thought that I might like an even bigger family, but I literally couldn't do another preganancy. So that's it for us. No more babies. We're finished. That ship has sailed.

Peter: It's left the dock and disappeared over the horizon, never to be seen again.

B is for Beaver Emojis

They say a picture tells a thousand words.

Well, not all pictures. Some pictures are a bit more direct than that, especially when Peter deploys them.

Enter the beaver emoji ...

Abbey: When we first got together, Pete was so romantic. He used to write me love notes. He'd go to work while I was still asleep, and when I woke up there'd be a little card on my pillow with a hand-written poem about how much he loved me and missed me when we were apart. I'd find them all over the place. On the table, in my bag, in the fridge. Sometimes there was a game where I had to follow a trail of love letters round the flat. A romantic treasure hunt with a beautiful poem as a prize. I have a large collection of Pete's poems in a box somewhere. Poetry Pete – who knew?

Peter: I was never the type to woo Abbey with a room full of flowers and balloons. That wasn't really my style. I'm not the Milk Tray bloke who arrives looking all smooth, dressed in a polo neck and armed with a big box of chocolates. But I did write poems. I used to really enjoy English at school, so I took to writing these little notes. They weren't half as bad as you might expect. Things were very simple back then. There was something quite lovely about those innocent times. Maybe I should get back into the habit of leaving those little notes everywhere. But life gets so complicated, doesn't it?

Abbey: And so now, Pete has a different way of communicating his feelings. He has discarded the pen in favour of the phone. Now, instead of writing poetry to express his deep and enduring love for me, he expresses his devotion through the medium of emojis.

Specifically: the beaver emoji. 🦫

And the aubergine emoji. 🍆

And the splash emoji. 💦

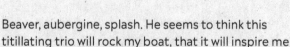

Beaver, aubergine, splash. He seems to think this titillating trio will rock my boat, that it will inspire me to sprint up the stairs and rip off his clothes.

Peter: I'm just putting my cards on the table. Life is short. We must grab every opportunity we can. When you have four children, you're never in the mood after you've finally put them all to bed, so you have to make your feelings clear whenever a window of opportunity, erm, arises. It seldom happens. There always seems to be someone in the house: builders on the scaffolding outside the window, the cleaner dusting outside our bedroom door. Sometimes it feels like we have to go on holiday, but you can't jet off to the Maldives every time you fancy a spot of beaver, aubergine, splash. So, when the time is right, you have to seize the moment. There's no time to compose a sonnet!

Abbey: But I'm sorry to report that the use of the beaver emoji has been known to backfire. Pete was at the golf club one evening and I wanted him to come home, so I sent him his favourite beaver emoji, knowing that he'd think, *I'm going to get lucky tonight!* I've never known him dash home so quickly. I suppose he was expecting to find me in my sexy underwear, awaiting his manly attentions. In fact, I was covered in fake tan with a face mask on, all ready to go to sleep.

Sorry, Pete.

Peter: In my book, that's entrapment. There needs to be a law against it. The beaver emoji is sacrosanct. You can only use it if you really, *really* mean it.

B is for irths

Ah, the miracle of birth. Whale music, scented candles, a husband lovingly wiping his wife's brow and whispering soft words of love and encouragement.

Or possibly not ...

Abbey: When Pete was playing football, my biggest fear was that I would go into labour naturally when he was playing at the other end of the country, or worse, somewhere in Europe. So for each of our four babies, I was induced to ensure that he could be there for the birth.

We developed a little routine. We'd stay at the Landmark hotel the night before, where we'd have a nice meal and watch some telly. In the morning we'd have a good breakfast (Rice Krispies for me, please), and head off to the Portland Hospital to give birth.

We documented the whole process on video for each of our four children: the journey to the hospital, the excitement on our apprehensive faces, and, as each of our beautiful little babies is born, me shrieking, 'IS IT ALIVE? IS IT OK? WHY HAVE YOU GOT THAT LOOK ON YOUR FACE? WHAT THE HELL'S WRONG?!'

Peter: Abbey is rightly proud of those videos. She was so sensational throughout each of her labours, it's like she was built to give birth. However, she'll put those home movies on for anybody who'll watch. *Anybody*. We have a large projector screen and she'll play it on that for the full immersive experience. The school mums seem to love it and get all emotional. The dads, though, don't half get a fright. I can't count the number of shivering, nauseous, pale-faced men I've seen retreating from that room, shaking their heads and muttering, 'Oh, my good God ...' My mates, my dad – they've all seen it in glorious technicolour.

Abbey: What we didn't film was you popping out to get yourself a peri-peri pitta from Nando's when my contractions were taking for ever, while I had nothing but some Lucozade energy sweets to see me through hours of labour.

Peter: A man's got to eat.

Abbey: I think God gave me straightforward labours to make up for the most horrendous pregnancies, but even so: with three of the births we got to a point where everything seemed to be proceeding so slowly that I'd send Pete out to the pub over the road for a pint, just to keep him occupied. Each time the barman would place the pint on the bar just as Pete's phone rang. 'Come back now, the baby's coming!' He didn't have a sip of any of those pints.

Peter: Which is evidence that we men also have our crosses to bear.

Abbey: And our hearts bleed for you. The least straightforward birth, though, was Liberty's, and that was more to do with Pete than with me, as he was in a bed by my side. He'd had a double hernia operation two weeks previously and, frankly, I was furious. Couldn't he have waited until after the birth? Apparently not.

Peter: In my defence, it was meant to be a routine operation. Lots of footballers have the same procedure without any problem. There's only supposed to be a tiny chance of anything going wrong – you'll feel a bit stiff on day one but will be walking around on day two. I thought I'd get it done and would be fine for the baby's arrival. Unfortunately, they put a mesh in my groin and it got infected. So as if not being able to go to the pub opposite wasn't bad enough, I also developed sepsis, a high temperature and was consigned to a hospital bed right next to Abbey.

Abbey: I was rolling around in agony trying to push out a baby while the nurses rushed around him, mopping his fevered brow, taking his temperature, dabbing him with a damp cloth. Every so often he'd groan, 'Alright, babe?' His great long arm would stretch out to give me a pat on the back of my hand. 'You keep going – you'll be alright!' And when I was recovering from labour with a vagina like a baboon's arse, there was no time for me to rest and recuperate with both of us out of action.

Peter: Perhaps, with hindsight, I *should* have waited until after the birth.

Abbey: I never wanted to find out the sex of any of our children. When I was pregnant for the third time, we already had two girls and Pete wanted to prepare himself for the possibility of a third. When the time came for the scan, we took Sophia with us. She and Pete were looking at the screen and I was blocking out all the chatter. I was only interested in knowing that the baby was healthy, and they were supposed to keep the sex a secret from me. But Sophia came over with a big smile on her face and said, 'Mum, you're going to be happy, *so* happy, because this time it's *different*!' So much for me not finding out.

I wouldn't have cared either way. I just love babies so much. Human babies, animal babies – anything baby and I'm there. I'd have another ten babies if I could only put up with the pregnancies. I love the way they look, the way they smell, the way they curl up asleep in your arms. I could look at a baby all day long.

Pete, on the other hand, thinks all babies look the same. They just look like babies. He doesn't get it when someone says, 'Ooh, he has his dad's eyes!' And I have to concede that I don't think any of my kids looked much like me when they were born. Johnny resembled a mixture of the turtle in *Finding Nemo* and Paul Daniels. In fact, a friend of mine thought he looked so *much* like Paul Daniels that he accidentally called him Paul for a while when he was first born. Which we liked, but not a lot.

Peter: When Jack was born, all you can hear on the video is: 'Is it alive? How big is it? *Has it got hair? IS IT GINGER?*'

I mean, I know I am a little bit of a ginge. Just a smidge. But what a question!

We were early out of the blocks when it came to babies. Abbey was only 25 when we had Sophia, and at one point we had three kids under the age of four. We had more double buggies, highchairs, car seats and little plastic Tupperwares of carrot sticks and juice boxes than you could shake a toddler at. To go anywhere was an operation more complicated than D-Day.

We were always determined, though, to make our babies live our lives with us. We laugh at some of our friends who seem to be exhausted by one baby, floored by parenting a single child. They can't go out because their child has to nap, they can't go to lunch - they can't even *eat* any lunch! - because little Maddison has to sleep in their own bed, with blackout blinds and Baby Mozart playing softly in the background, and Mummy has to snooze with baby just to make up for the early start that morning.

Try doing that with four children and you wouldn't leave the house for the next decade. You'd want to punch Mozart's lights out. Our children can sleep anywhere, through anything - weddings, bar mitzvahs, maybe not funerals - as we wanted to carry on our lives. Perhaps it's one of the advantages of being younger, fitter and firmer when we had them ...

But there's never a perfect time to have a baby. You're never where you want to be. Nobody ever regrets it, though.

B is for bonkbeats

Picture the scene. The lights are low, the champagne is on ice, romance is in the air. You both know where the evening is leading. So one of you sidles over to your phone, cranks up Spotify and selects something sultry to fire things along.

That's the bonkbeat. And nothing could be sexier, right? Wrong.

Peter: A listener wrote in with a problem. Her husband favoured a nice, slow Susan Boyle ballad as a bonkbeat, whereas she fancied raving between the sheets to Swedish House Mafia. I mean, each to their own. You do you, sexy Susan Boyle/Swedish House Mafia couple. But it got me thinking: which songs would be in the list of top five bonkbeats? And that got me thinking even harder: who the hell wants a bonkbeat anyway? What would Abbey's reaction be if I stepped over to the record player with a meaningful glint in my eye to spin *Barry White's Greatest Hits* to get her in the mood? Would the Walrus of Love add some spice to proceedings?

Absolutely not. I honestly think Abbey would projectile vomit if I did that, and I wouldn't blame her ...

Abbey: Are we really going to talk about this? Because if we are, full disclosure: Peter coyly hasn't mentioned the time a bonkbeat got into his head. Things were getting hot and steamy, there happened to be music on in the background, and I suddenly noticed that he was – how can I put this delicately? – moving to the rhythm. As soon as I realised what he was doing, the moment was gone and I laughed my head off ...

Peter: Which is just what you want, isn't it, to be laughed at during sex? But in my book, randomly having music on in the background is a whole different ball game to actively choosing a bit of bump and grind to get your partner in the mood. That would make me feel very uncomfortable. There's no bigger cringe than the idea of someone playing 'Let's Get It On' and *taking the lyrics literally!* Surely there's no situation in which that wouldn't be a terminal passion-killer ...

And it would be even worse if I let my Spotify algorithm take over. Because like every parent, my Spotify homepage is a mash-up of dinosaur rhymes and teeny pop. I look at my recommendations and I hardly even know who I am anymore. Imagine the excruciating moment when you think you're going to get lucky to 'Can't Get Enough of Your Love, Babe', only for the moment to be catastrophically ruined by the *Hey Duggee* soundtrack.

Abbey: We had family over to stay at our place in Portugal, and rather than sit up drinking into the small hours, Peter and I headed upstairs, totally intending to go to sleep. But Peter's phone was still connected to the speaker downstairs, and it randomly started playing 'Sexual Healing'. So you can imagine what our family thought was happening. They couldn't have been further from the truth. I had a face mask on and Peter was tucked up in his PJs watching the golf. I still don't know what was worse – that they thought we'd slipped upstairs for a crafty shag, or that we were a bonkbeating couple in the first place ...

I'd rather put *Grey's Anatomy* on pause – preferably on a scene that doesn't include a hot girl – and do it in silence. Then we can put the telly back on and have a nice cup of tea and a biscuit. Perfect.

Peter: So bonkbeats are a hard no from us. Susan Boyle has no place in the Crouch–Clancy bedroom. Which means that rather than choosing our favourite bonkbeats, we present a count down of our top five absolute worst, passion-killing, ick-inducing bonkbeats of all time.

5 'Freak Me' by Another Level (instant passion killer)

4 'Bump n' Grind' by R Kelly (I think we can all agree that R Kelly's off the menu)

3 'Sexual Healing' by Marvin Gaye (just ... no)

2 'I Dreamed a Dream' by Susan Boyle (the mind boggles)

1 'Don't You Worry Child' by Swedish House Mafia (why would anyone think this is a good idea?)

Agony ~~Aunt~~ Ab

Dear Abbey,

I wanted to seek your advice regarding couple dynamics in our friendship group. Recently two of our best friends split after a long relationship. Before they split, we did absolutely everything together as a group: nights out, weekends away, parties at our place.

However, since the split we don't know how we will be able to get together as a group ever again. Both of them are our friends and it'd be very hard to pick one over the other, but something needs to happen, as the group without them is nowhere near as good.

Freddy, 31 – Dublin

Abbey: I know what this feels like. When a couple you are friends with have been together for a long time and then split up, you go into a state of mourning. It's like there's been a death in the family. If someone has had a really big presence in a group when they are on nights out or on holiday, it can feel like something is really missing when they are no longer there.

Usually when a couple splits up they never want to see each other again, so it's unlikely they're both going to be hanging out with the group of friends again, but if you invite one and not the other you'll always run the risk of upsetting someone.

Peter: Could you see them alternate nights, one night with one and the next night with the other? After a couple of weeks of doing that you'd soon work out who is the fun one and then you can cut the other one loose.

Abbey: Who do you think our friends would like more, out of us, if we split up?

Peter: A lot of the people we hang out with and go to things like Glastonbury with are your family, so I'd say I'd be the one cut! I think if there's one person going out for someone's birthday, it'd be you, not me.

Abbey: I actually think it's the other way round: my family would prefer you, but I think our friends would prefer me.

Peter: Baby, it's a tough one, but let's hope we stay together. For that reason.

C

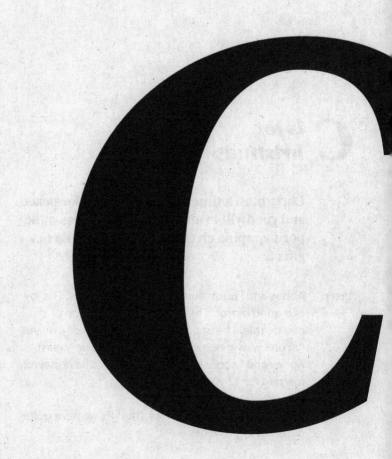

C is for hristmas

Christmas: a time for hope and joy, for peace and goodwill to all men, for Christmas milk, pornographic elves and hideous emergency gifts ...

Peter: Abbey and I normally agree on most things. The joy of a good buffet. The correct interpretation of the offside rule. The importance of golf. Actually, maybe I'm on my own here. I'll try again. At the very least, Abbey and I agree on enough things to have stayed married for 12 years and counting.

When it comes to Christmas, though, we have quite different approaches.

In our household, Christmas kicks off in November. Abbey would go earlier if she could. October certainly. June given half the chance. In fact, I sometimes wonder if she wouldn't be happier leaving the Christmas stuff out all year round. It's like *Home Alone* with all the decorations and lights, which start at the gate, cover the trees and adorn the length of the drive.

Abbey: As you can probably tell, Pete's not one of those blokes who goes out in his checked flannel shirt with his sleeves rolled up to hack down a Christmas tree and carry it over his shoulder through the snow. He's not queuing up outside the butchers on Christmas Eve to collect the turkey. Being six-foot-seven, he *is* quite useful at putting the star on the top of the tree, and he's not too bad at picking up the wrapping paper and putting it in a bin bag on Christmas Day. But, frankly, he simply comes home one evening to see the decorations up and the planning done, and he says, 'Oh! Is it Christmas?'

Peter: Abbey loves all the little details. The whole family comes over to us for Christmas, and she will have us all in matching pyjamas with our names on. She'll spend ages collecting the perfect little gifts for the kids' stockings, and thoughtful presents for everyone else. Each present will be beautifully wrapped in personalised wrapping paper. Everything is perfect, she's in charge, and it means that over the festive period I have only two jobs.

Abbey: Peter's first festive job is Elf on the Shelf. Unfortunately, his sense of humour demands that I'll be called to have a look at how he's posed the elf, only to find it standing behind a Barbie doll on all fours with Susan Boyle playing in the background (see B is for Bonkbeats). Frankly, if the kids saw Elfie and Barbie going at it doggy style – they'd be traumatised for life.

Peter: It is true that I like to be creative with my Elf on the Shelf choices, but I make sure the elf buttons up his fly in time to set up the kid-friendly version for the morning. It's quite a responsibility, actually, because when we first got the elf we realised the kids were rather scared of it, freaked out by the idea that it might creep upstairs while they were asleep. We had to persuade them that the elf couldn't cope with stairs, like a Dalek.

My second festive job is the acquisition of Abbey's present. This is not a straightforward procedure.

I like to do my shopping the old-school way: by going to the shops in a blind panic on Christmas Eve. Because that's what Christmas is all about, isn't it? It's a battle out there, with all the other men frantically searching, sweating, smelling a bit of the fortifying lunchtime pint they downed to prepare themselves for the fight. What could be more festive than glancing at the panic-purchase of one of your Christmas Eve comrades and thinking, *He's having a 'mare – she's gonna hate that ...*

Abbey drops hints, at least she tells me she does. But they must be too subtle for me to interpret, as I seem to get it wrong every year. She tells me I should ask her mum or sister what she'd like, as they're the ones who know her best. But I want the present to be from me, something *I've* taken the care to choose.

Big mistake.

It's become a bit of a thing. A moment. The whole room stops when the time comes for her to open the present from me. Everybody wants front-row seats. *What's he done this time? How bad can it be? Worse than last year? Surely that's impossible* ... The whole family is glued to the action. Think World Cup final penalty shoot-out levels of tension. They're silent, mouths open, breath held. How terrible is Dad's present going to be?

Abbey: Let it not be forgotten that you bought me the same Burberry mac three years in a row.

Peter: This is true. It's the action of a man in a panic, isn't it? Each time I saw it, I must have thought, *That's perfect! It's classy, she's classy. It's glamorous, she's glamorous*. Unfortunately, I must have had the same thought every year for three years in a row. I honestly had no recollection of buying it previously. And I was tragically pleased with myself three times in a row, too. *That's brilliant*, I thought thrice. *I've nailed it!*

Abbey: Last year's present was particularly special. A tiny box, beautifully wrapped. I was excited. What could it be? A necklace? A ring? Surely not a diamond? I unwrapped it with trembling fingers to find ... a two-metre-long phone-charging cable. What more could a girl dream of?

Peter: I put a lot of thought into that present. I observed that you're always on your phone but are often running out of charge. I observed that you can't charge it from your side of the bed. It's not a high-value gift, but does that level of thoughtfulness count for nothing?

Abbey: I'll tell you what does count for nothing. The year I *got* nothing. Not one thing. I gave Pete loads of little presents. He gave me zilch.

Peter: What's a guy to do? I'd asked, 'What do you want for Christmas?' She'd replied, 'Babe, let's not do presents this year. It's too much. Christmas is just for the kids.'

You live and learn. I now know that 'Let's not do presents' means 'You definitely need to get a present, just a different type of present'. It's a minefield, and you need to be a mind reader. Does she want presents? Does she not want presents? What sort of presents? I get it wrong most of the time, and sometimes she ends up in tears. *You don't even know me. Why would you buy me this?*

When she was pregnant with Sophia, I bought her a baby blanket, which I thought she would love. She most definitely didn't ...

Abbey: It was a baby-blue blanket, and we didn't even know the sex of the baby! He also bought me a maroon Anya Hindmarch baby-changing bag. It was lovely, but fellas, a word of advice. Don't ever buy your wife a pregnancy-related Christmas present. Get us something a little bit glamorous that makes us feel like everything isn't just about being a baby-growing machine.

Peter: Like a pair of leather hotpants?

Abbey: Which you bought me when I was *six months pregnant* and about *twenty stone*. I couldn't even get them over my thigh. Still can't. But even the hot pants were better than the bright orange Chanel bumbag that made me look like a bumblebee.

Peter: I was taken advantage of by the shop assistant! It was 5.25pm on Christmas Eve and she saw me coming, covered in sweat, white panic on my face. I'm picking up bags, looking at prices, thinking, *Jesus Christ!* and putting them back down. And the shop assistant clearly thought, *Here's the mug who left it till closing time on Christmas Eve. I haven't been able to shift this old junk for years, but I reckon I can flog this loser literally anything.* 'This is limited edition. It's very chic, very fashionable, the colour is very rare. It's very Chanel, a signature look ...'

Chic, fashionable, rare – what's not to love?

Abbey: It's still in its box.

Happily, though, Christmas isn't just about presents. When all the Christmas decorating and shopping is done, there's only one thing left for me to do to capture the Christmas spirit. I sit down and have a Baileys, or a 'Christmas milk', as we called it in my house. Every Christmas my nan would wrap up a bottle, put it under the tree and say, 'I've got you a bottle of Baileys.' It never was real Baileys, but that didn't matter. It became a tradition, and that's what Christmas is really all about: being cosy and snuggling up together at home as a family. It's the best feeling. I've never wanted to spend Christmas anywhere else.

Peter: We did go to the Maldives for ten days before Christmas once, but we flew back to the UK for Christmas Day and Boxing Day, before flying back on holiday on the 27th. We just couldn't bear not to be at home, waking up super-early, asking if Santa's been ...

Abbey: Pretending we had nothing to do with the stockings and looking surprised that Santa could possibly have known to bring the perfect present.

Peter: And when else do you get to drink champagne and orange juice at 7.30 in the morning?

It's a far cry from the Christmases I had when I was playing football. Everybody else was off work and footballers were the entertainment. We'd train on Christmas Day and play on Boxing Day, so I wouldn't normally even *have* a Christmas. The same went for New Year's Eve, which I'd normally spend tucked up in a Novotel watching the telly on my own.

Abbey: Which somehow makes it all the more special. I'm a regular Mrs Christmas, always trying to make it special for everybody. It's by far my favourite day of the year, and not even an emergency orange bumbag can change that.

C is for cravings

Coal, tar, chocolate, seaweed, shoe leather, peanut butter and pickles – whatever a pregnant woman craves, God forbid any man fails to supply it. And it really doesn't matter if it's unavailable, undesirable or even downright inedible ...

Peter: Ever heard of Goblin Pie? Me neither. Turns out it's a little suet pudding in a tin that makes Fray Bentos look like a three-star Michelin blow-out. Abbey used to eat Goblin Pie when she was little, and when she was pregnant that's what she wanted. Actually, not wanted. *Needed*. No matter that it was the Pedigree Chum of pre-packaged pie. It *had* to be Goblin. She would accept no substitute.

Now, I don't want to mansplain pregnancy cravings. Poor Abbey had hyperemesis gravidarum, like the

Princess of Wales. It's a chronic form of morning sickness that saw Abbey projectile vomit all day, every day. I was glad she wanted to eat anything at all, even if it was dog-food pie. But I was surprised. I thought that the pregnant body was supposed to choose the really good stuff to grow a strong and healthy baby. Apparently not. Abbey just wanted cheap meat packed with hormones that would otherwise usually repulse her. She *craved* Goblin Pie.

So I hunted for it. I looked high and low. No luck. I thought, *Maybe it's a northern thing,* so I tried asking around in Liverpool. No joy. Not a Goblin Pie to be found. Eventually I tracked down the factory where it was made. Feeling enormously pleased with myself, I called them up. Then ... disaster! I learned that they'd stopped making Goblin Pie because the packaging cost more than the ingredients, which says a lot about what was in it.

I'm sorry to report that Abbey received this news badly. Her craving wasn't going to be sated by the minor inconvenience of the foodstuff no longer existing. I retreated, tail tucked, from the explosion and pleaded with the manufacturers: 'I'll give you anything, whatever you want, for you to open up the factory and start making the pies again. *Please, I'm begging you! Anything!*'

But they wouldn't. And Abbey was wailing, 'If you really loved me, you'd get me a Goblin Pie!'

'But Abs—'

'The fact that you haven't *proves* that you don't love me!'

'I can get you one from the chippy. Steak and kidney. It's cheap and nasty. You'll love it!'

'It's not the same! You don't love me! You don't even *know* me!'

Abbey: I can't believe I behaved like that, especially over a Goblin Pie. I normally love healthy, home-cooked food, and make a mean shepherd's pie myself. But when I was pregnant I didn't want anything of the sort. I wanted the nastiest, most highly processed ready-made version available. Pete didn't get it. One day he sweetly went out to buy me a high-end shepherd's pie, made with fillet steak and a red wine jus. I couldn't stomach it. I wanted the £1 microwave version with questionable meat and no discernible flavour.

Peter: We were at a school sports day and Abbey wanted a prawn sandwich, so I popped to M&S and found their 'world's finest prawn sandwich'. The world's finest! I'd absolutely nailed it. I walked back to Abbey with a chuffed grin on my face and presented her with this splendid feast. 'There you go, babe. World's finest.'

She looked at the sandwich. She looked at me. Then she broke down in tears and wailed, 'How can I be having a baby with a man who gets it this wrong?'

Abbey: I was in floods of tears. The whole school was watching us, thinking, *They must have had a right old barney.* My reaction was so over the top, as if I'd received terrible personal news. But in fact I was just a crazy woman crying because I didn't *want* the M&S one with Marie Rose dressing and crispy iceberg lettuce. I wanted – needed – a cheap, basic, bog-standard prawn sandwich from the garage. I wanted the Goblin Pie of sandwiches.

Peter: It's hard, as a man, watching your wife lose it over a prawn sandwich. I tried to adjust my thinking, but just when I thought I'd cracked it, she moved on to a new craving. She'd want the same thing for 15 days in a row, and I'd bring it to her on day 16 only to be met with dagger eyes. 'How dare you? I hate this now!'

Abbey: But one constant craving was a night-time McFlurry. Pete used to think nothing of going out at 2am to get me one. He was like Jim Dear in *Lady and the Tramp*, going out in the freezing snow to get food for Darling.

How times change. These days, if I ask Pete to bring me up a cup of tea he turns into Kevin the Teenager. Gone are the days when he used to drive 40 minutes for a McFlurry. Now he won't even make me a cup of tea with the hot tap!

Peter: I'd still go to the services for you, babe. Who says romance is dead?

But full disclosure: even when Abbey is not pregnant, I have to watch my step. She likes biscuits in bed. One night she'll say, 'Bring me two, Pete.' So I'll bring her two, and she'll say, 'Are you trying to make me fat?' So the next night I'll bring her one, and she'll say, 'Why have I only got one? Do you think I'm fat?'

We sportsmen sometimes have to accept when we're beaten, and this is a game I simply cannot win.

D

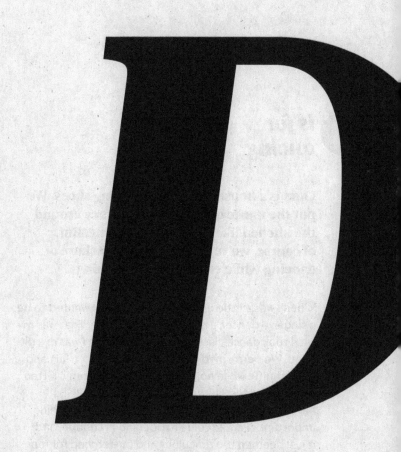

D is for Dancing

Ours is a house filled with dancing shoes. We put the music on – loud – and dance around the kitchen like nobody is watching. But, of course, we've also done our fair share of dancing while *everybody* is watching ...

Abbey: When I was a little girl, I always said that I wanted to be a singer, a dancer, a model and an actress. That was my list. I took dance classes as a kid, and then I was in a girl band. We performed a very basic two-step, a left and right shuffle while holding our mics like Atomic Kitten. Hardly a full NSYNC dance routine. And while I'd have loved to pursue that kind of career, everything important seemed to be happening in London, and it just seemed too ridiculous and far-fetched for me even to consider going for it. I suffered from a serious lack of confidence, which is not something I ever want my own kids to experience.

Even now I'm shy and can get anxious in front of a crowd, so when I was first asked to be on *Strictly Come Dancing* I refused. I knew exactly how hard it would be. They kept asking me, and I kept saying no. I must have turned them down four times. I just didn't think I could face it. Then my manager accepted the offer without asking me first. When he told me what he'd done, I thought to myself, *OK … it's time to do this!*

My favourite part of doing *Strictly* was the training. I loved the music, I loved the dancing and it made me feel fabulous. Dance training isn't like going to the gym, where you're running on a treadmill and staring at a screen for hours on end. I was constantly learning a new skill and I love to learn new things. You're in a bubble with all the other contestants, and I'd spend my life there laughing and happy.

But I hated the live performance on Saturday night. I would feel physically ill, sick with nerves. Those performances were harder than I ever anticipated. I wanted to be brilliant, but I wasn't. In my mind I was Ginger Rogers, and it was so frustrating to see that what I was doing with my body bore no relation at all to what I was trying to create in my head. When you're young, everyone tells you to dance like nobody's watching. The trouble with being on *Strictly* is that *everybody's* watching, and there's nothing quite like having to look at yourself replayed on a TV screen to make you feel like a massive twat.

I won the competition. It sounds easy to say it, but the truth is that I spent most of the time feeling disappointed in myself. I knew I could have done it ten times better if I'd only been able to get over my nerves, and I felt like everybody was so much better than me. Some were proper dancers and had been to dance college. Some were pop stars and were used to being on stage and learning complicated choreography. There were actors and TV hosts, confident in front of a crowd. I'm not great with all eyes on me, and the intense pressure would really get to me. I'm the exact opposite to Pete in that respect. He's amazing in front of a crowd and really loves an audience. I suppose playing every game of football in front of 40,000 people helps. He thrives off the energy and affirmation of an audience. The bigger the crowd, the bolder he gets, whereas I just want to shrink and disappear.

So why did I win? I honestly think it's because I went on the biggest 'journey'. The public loves a journey and mine was the most dramatic. I'd come a long way from where I started. (When the live tour came around, I still managed to balls it up every night!)

I don't miss *Strictly* too much. It was an incredible experience while it lasted, but it's not real life. I've had three babies since then, which feels mad, and while I think I could probably still fit into some of my dresses, you're not allowed to keep them. They get recycled for next year or broken down for sequins. It can feel like a bit of a shame but it's good for the environment.

Peter: Of course, Abbey's not the only one in the house who has form when it comes to dancing, although I'm not sure if The Robot would impress the *Strictly* judges. It came out of a moment of pure madness. I was at a party at David Beckham's house and everyone was on the dance floor, including a camera crew. For a laugh, I shouted, 'Watch this!' at my Liverpool teammates and shimmied past the camera crew doing weird robotic dance moves. Don't ask me why. Everyone was in tears laughing, and David Beckham asked if he could keep the footage, which ended up on TV the next day. My teammates made me promise to do the dance next time I scored for England. I kept the promise and The Robot went mainstream.

I only did The Robot three times on the pitch, but now it's a regular at parties. There are kids who weren't even born when I first did it, who I now see busting the same move. Even walking through Glastonbury 20 years later, every few minutes we'd hear someone shout out, 'Oi, Pete, can we see The Robot?!'

And weirdly, even though I had a twenty-year football career, scored a hundred goals and have a wall full of England caps, our kids think I'm most famous for being a judge on *The Masked Dancer*. I was retired by the time they had any concept of who I was, so they've never been all that interested in my football career. Their mum on *Strictly*, though? Different story.

Abbey: Dancing's always been part of our lives. After my first date with Pete we got a taxi home and he started dancing – and I mean *really* dancing – in the back of the cab. I don't think he's ever really stopped since. We constantly have music on, and the kids are always having a little dance around the kitchen before school with Pete and me. When we first moved into our house we didn't have any rugs or furniture, so we decided to throw a massive party and ended up having a breakdancing competition in the living room. It descended into dance chaos, with everyone pulling each other across the slippery new wooden floors and finally putting on furry coats to zoom across the floor.

And our family motto? 'If you're not grooving, you're losing.' Words to live by, if you ask me.

D is for ating

For Peter and Abbey, it all started with a romantic argument outside the loo. But happily they never had to swipe right (or is it left?).

Peter: I'll always put it down as the luckiest day of my life. I broke my drought of goals at Liverpool, having played in 18 matches without bothering the score sheet. My much-needed goal came from the lamest strike, but it went in and that's what matters. And I scored again that evening when I met Abbey at a club. Normally I struggle even to pull a hamstring, but like I said, this was the luckiest day of my life. I should have picked my lottery numbers that night too.

Abbey: I saw him standing there by the toilet. I knew who he was, which makes it sound like I was stalking him, but I really wasn't. I'd just seen him being teased a bit in the press, and he looked like such a lovely man. So I fancied him before I saw him in real life, and when we met I fancied him all the more. I don't know what it was about him, but I felt like he needed looking after. He seemed like a fish out of water, and I found that endearing. OK, so he needed a bit of a makeover. The hair possibly needed some attention. The clothes definitely did. In fact, the whole package required a bit of TLC, but that wasn't a problem. I reckoned I could work with the raw materials. I gave him my number and I remember going to the loo thinking, *This is the guy*. I knew from day one that I'd found him.

When I came back from the loo, though, he was talking to another girl. Already! I walked straight up to him and said, 'You just asked me for my number and now you're talking to another girl. What sort of bloke are you?'

Peter: That was our first row, and we weren't even going out yet!

I was leaving for Japan in the next few days, and Abbey was going straight on to *Britain's Next Top Model*. It meant we were apart for quite a while at the very beginning, but they do say that absence makes the heart grow fonder. We spent most of that time on the phone to each other. We talked every day.

Abbey: When the time came for our first date, I didn't want to tell my mum and dad, but I was only 19 and had absolutely no money whatsoever. So I told my parents I was going to see my friend Kate and asked them for £10 for the taxi. 'Don't waste your money,' Mum said, and she offered to drive me. I felt so awful lying, but in the end Pete collected me from the end of the road. He took me to this old man's pub opposite his flat.

I worried that his plan was to get me pissed and then take me back to his place and put the bonkbeats on. Maybe he already had the tunes lined up, his Susan Boyle CD already sitting in the player. But I wanted to take things slowly. The bonkbeats would have to wait.

Halfway through the evening, Pete went to the toilet and I offered to buy him a drink. I had no idea how much drinks cost, especially beer. At that time if you were a girl on a night out in Liverpool, you'd start the evening with £20 in your pocket and finish it with £15. Drinks were always bought for you, and the only thing you needed to spend money on was the bus fare home. I was so nervous about not having enough money that I ordered a pint of Guinness for Pete and a glass of tap water for myself. He was a bit confused when he came back – he thought I didn't drink much, which was more unusual back then.

Peter: From that point on, everything was a bit of a whirlwind. Suddenly, Abbey was in the public eye because of *Britain's Next Top Model*, and that made everything more intense. It's hard enough finding your way as boyfriend and girlfriend at a young age. But to find your picture everywhere and to have your private life written about in the newspapers was really quite weird. I was used to being the 'beanpole' player, of course, and only too familiar with public discussions about my performance on the pitch. But nothing prepared me for people wanting to know about my relationships or my life away from football. Nobody had ever really looked at me in that way before.

Abbey: I had zero experience of that kind of attention, and I definitely wasn't looking for it. I went into *Britain's Next Top Model* because I wanted to model. I didn't expect to become well known and hadn't even thought about fame. Nowadays, when people sign up to reality TV series, they already have huge Instagram followings and are ready-made influencers. Everything was different back then. I was just an ordinary girl, and the reality of being known hit me like a ton of bricks.

Peter: Likewise. I just wanted to play football and would have been happy to do it at any level. I wasn't interested in anything else.

Abbey: The day I finished *Britain's Next Top Model*, I drove straight home. When Pete called and asked me if I wanted to come to Portugal with the England team before the World Cup in Germany, I told him I couldn't go. It was a world I wasn't used to and I had six weeks' worth of dirty laundry in a suitcase in the hall with no cash to go and buy swanky designer clothes. Talk about self-conscious. More to the point, Pete and I still didn't really know each other that well. He'd been in Japan and I'd been filming for six weeks. But, after some faffing, I gave myself a good talking-to and thought, *To hell with it*. I decided to go. I sped down the M62 and they held the plane for me.

Peter: I felt sorry for Abbey. She was super-young and there she was amidst this circus. It takes a while to get comfortable around someone you like, and we had to do it in the public eye.

Abbey: It was weird for my family too. In Liverpool, football culture is everything. Everyone lives for Liverpool or Everton. So for a Liverpool and England player to walk into my house was extraordinary, verging on the ridiculous. We'd come home and there would be ten little kids sitting on the sofa, my brother John's friends from school, their legs swinging excitedly, all waiting to have a look at him. Rather than staring sweetly or gawping with their mouths open and saying nothing, this lot pelted him with questions and asked him to sign stuff and to have a photograph with them. John still has a picture of Pete on his wall, even though he's part of the family now. Our relationship made him a bit of a celebrity at school.

My sister's experience wasn't so positive. She was bullied, even by teachers, who'd say things like, 'I've seen that Abbey in the papers today, what does she think she's wearing?' One teacher read out an article in front of the whole class for a good old laugh. My sister was really embarrassed and developed anxiety, and Pete and I had to go into the school and ask them to stop drawing so much attention to her.

Peter: We've been together now for such a long time that we've not had to be on the dating scene in ages. Frankly, I'm glad to be out of it. I'm not sure either of us would survive out there on the dating savannah. There are too many apex predators for a couple of unseasoned prey like us.

Abbey: We get questions about dating all the time on our podcast, which the pair of us are totally ill-equipped to answer because we're so out of touch. Neither of us has ever been on a dating app. We're complete technophobes who can barely switch on our own TV, so the idea of setting up a dating profile is completely beyond us. What would happen if nobody swiped right? (Or is it left?) And then, once you've gone to the trouble of starting to chat in the app, how do you know that people really are who they say they are?

Peter: You don't. A mate of mine was properly catfished on Instagram the other day. This girl sent him a gorgeous photo of herself and said she was keen to meet up. He agreed, the fool! I've been out of the dating game for years, but even I know that if it looks too good to be true, it probably is. She turned up to the date looking nothing like her photo, which serves him right! Rookie error. Don't go dating randoms from Instagram.

Abbey: I wouldn't know where to begin even if I wanted to. I can't even put restrictions on my children's iPhone, let alone fiddle around with the settings on a dating app. All the rules that I grew up with – like taking relationships slowly if you really like someone – seem very old-fashioned now. I'm no prude, but I've seen stuff online that I'd never do.

So, all in all, I'm delighted to no longer be part of the dating game. It feels so much more difficult than it was in our day. People expect everything to be perfect so quickly. I can't imagine anyone putting up with Pete's awful, fetid flat, or being attracted to my orange tan and hair extensions. And social media means that all your mistakes are out there for everyone to see. It's as if we're expected to arrive fully formed in the dating world, with our edges rubbed smooth – and that's simply not how it is when you're young.

I'd be useless out there. Utterly useless!

D is for Diamonds

It's a footballer thing, isn't it, the diamonds and the bling? Ice in the earlobes and a rock as big as your eyeball for your wife or girlfriend.

A diamond is a beautiful thing, we're told. A precious gift from one partner to another to symbolise the deep, sparkling beauty of the relationship, its eternal nature, its inability to be crushed under pressure ...

Peter: Bollocks. I said to Abbey one day, 'I don't believe in diamonds.'

Abbey: To which I replied, 'What does that even mean? How can you not "believe" in diamonds? They're not the Tooth Fairy.'

Peter: What it means is, diamonds are a load of shite. Pretty enough, I suppose, but why would you spend all that money on something that just hangs off your body and doesn't enrich your life in any way? The engagement ring, I understand: a symbol of your love. But the consistent, repeated purchasing of diamonds? Absolutely ridiculous when you think about what else you could spend that money on. A holiday, an adventure ...

Abbey: Wise words here from the man who spent his entire life savings joining a golf club.

Peter: And think how much fun I'm going to have there! Think of all the smiles and enjoyment it's going to bring me. Blow that cash on a diamond and you forget about it the moment it's dangling from your ear. And men wearing diamonds? If you're a rapper you can just about pull it off, but a footballer? Not that it stops some of the lads. There's this one bloke who is the footballer's jeweller, procurer of diamonds to the Premier League. He's been trying to sell me a diamond since I was 18, and I'd never bought anything from him. 'One day,' he told me, 'I'm going to get you.' But he never did, apart from once, when Abbey gave me a drawing of what she wanted her engagement ring to look like. For that purpose, this jeweller was the man. But outside of engagement rings, I just don't believe in the things.

Abbey: You can get people's ashes made into diamonds – did you know that? I guess I'm going to have to wait until Peter snuffs it before I can get my ten carat. But if I had it made from his ashes, he'd always be with me, round my little finger.

Or, some might say, under my thumb ...

D is for DIY

Who doesn't like a man who's good with his hands? Who doesn't like to look out of the window and see a shirtless hunk with a leather tool belt mending the garden fence? A man who can build a Wendy house for his daughter as she sleeps? A man who can hold the car up with one hand while fixing a tyre with the other? A man who can glue a handle back on to a broken mug, or even just change a light bulb?

Abbey: Peter has many strengths. He's an amazing father, an incredible husband, a fabulous footballer, a great pundit and the best friend. He plays a decent round of golf, he's excellent at drinking a pint, he's got killer dance moves (so long as The Robot, over and over again, is your thing).

But DIY? It's just not one of his skills. Can he wire a plug? I suspect not. Can he change a light bulb? Just about. But we all have to stand around and admire his handiwork once he's done it, and maybe give him a little clap as he proudly switches the light on and off.

Peter: It's true. DIY is just not my forte. But, you know, I bet those people who are good at DIY would much rather be good at football. You can't have it all, can you?

I do *wish* I was good at it, though. I'd love to be able to assemble a bit of IKEA furniture without being left with 65 screws in the bag that should have gone somewhere and then losing my temper with the stupid thing! There's nothing I'd like more than to be able to chop down a Christmas tree and haul it home through the forest to the sound of 'Driving Home for Christmas'. Sadly, in that respect, I'm not your man.

I think all guys *should* have a basic understanding of DIY, but unfortunately my skills are limited to changing the batteries in the kids' toys. I feel very proud of myself, unscrewing the little bit of plastic, popping in a new battery, screwing it back on again while the kids stand in awe at my astonishing technical prowess. I've even got a toolbox for that very job, like a real man.

The hard truth is that the kids have loads of toys that aren't quite right because I don't have the skills to build them properly. So I have to make up excuses. 'Of course that castle doesn't have a door on it. It's because they live in a hot country!' 'That's not a quad, it's a trike!' They seem happy enough with my feeble explanations.

Abbey: So, in the absence of a husband who's handy with a screwdriver, we have our friend Robin. Thank goodness for Robin! He can do anything. When we have a barbecue, it's Robin who has to bring round the gas. If something round the house needs doing, Robin's our guy.

And when Robin's not around, and the kids need help with a homework that requires some sort of practical ability, I have to step in. I've made three separate Stonehenges now. I got an A for the last one that I made out of Bourbon biscuits.

Peter: Well-deserved. Abbey and I have talked about going on various courses for self-improvement, and DIY is one of them. I'd like to learn how to fix things, cook things and speak a foreign language. Unfortunately, I'm useless at all of them. The only foreign language I speak is the embarrassing one we Brits sometimes lapse into when we just speak loudly in English with a dodgy foreign accent. I'd love to be good at all this stuff, for my tombstone to say, 'Chef, linguist, DIY ninja'.

Abbey: Never going to happen.

D is for Do Him Up

It's a truth universally acknowledged that most men need a bit of a tweak at the beginning of a relationship, just to smooth over the rough edges and bring them up to scratch.

Abbey: Pete certainly needed a little bit of polishing when we first got together. He might have been a Liverpool and England player, but his skills with the boot weren't quite reflected in his dress sense. To be frank, he dressed like an Inbetweener. Half-mast pants, Puma trainers tied so tight that both sides were closed up, a big baggy jumper that was too short in the arms.

But he had that beautiful face, and those kind eyes. The raw materials were there, and I knew I had something to work with. This wouldn't be a disaster.

It would only take a little bit of tweaking to bring out the best in him.

The secret, ladies, is to move softly, without causing offence. The last thing we want to do is make our guy feel self-conscious, or like they have no style. Thoughtful gifts can be a powerful weapon in our armoury. A nice pair of pants that actually fit. A stylish pair of shoes.

To be fair, I was lucky that Peter only needed simple tweaks. So many of my friends fall for guys who are the polar opposite of what they're into. They get with a man who has a shaved head and no stubble, when what they really like is long hair and a beard. That's a much bigger project to tackle, and harder to achieve by stealth.

Peter: I don't think I realised I was being tweaked at the time. I just knew that Abbey was stylish and that I didn't really like clothes shopping. So, if she takes care of my wardrobe, everyone's a winner, right?

Abbey: It's kind of Peter to say I was stylish, but back then I absolutely wasn't. I *was*, however, more stylish than him. Which wasn't hard. Even now I can't control my laughter when he goes shopping and comes back with the world's most tragic outfits. Outfits that make people stop and stare, and not for the right reasons. He just can't be trusted in a clothes shop.

Peter: But what it means is that now, in my old age, I've developed a secret love of clothes shopping, because it feels like I'm going rogue ...

Abbey: The lovely thing about Peter now is that he's almost fully house-trained. He's learned to put his shoes away rather than leave them in the hall, and the floordrobe is almost - *almost* - a thing of the past. The days of him eating a bag of crisps and then wiping his fingers on the couch are behind us. We have the occasional relapse when he leaves his dirty undies and socks on the floor, but if Pete were to be passed on to another woman, like a rescue puppy, I believe that they would be pleased with his training.

Peter: I've been taught well, and have worked tirelessly to get where I am today. It's been a long, hard slog but the effort is paying dividends.

Abbey: Maybe he's been taught *too* well. Maybe I've broken the first rule of doing your man up, which is: don't let him go above a six out of ten. Make him *too* stylish, *too* well house-trained, and he might start to attract the gaze of other women. And we don't want that! The honest truth is that Pete's a solid ten, so maybe I *should* let him go shopping by himself a little more often ...

Agony ~~Aunt~~ Ab

Dear Abbey,

For a long time I've felt like my marriage was missing something. After listening to your podcast, I now have a good idea what it might be: my wife lacks any taste whatsoever when it comes to what to watch on the box.

Not only does she bring no recommendations to the table when we're endlessly scrolling through Netflix, she also has zero appreciation for the absolute belters I am pulling out of the bag on a regular basis.

Succession, *The Sopranos*, *Breaking Bad* and *Peaky Blinders* are just a few of the game changers that I have introduced her to over the years. Meanwhile, all I get in return is *Keeping Up with the Kardashians* and *The Real Housewives of* pissing *Orange County*.

This wouldn't be so much of a problem if I received the recognition that I so clearly deserve for bringing such groundbreaking works of art into her life. Whenever we finish a series, though, the most I can expect in terms of feedback is, 'That was alright,' or, 'Is that it?'

Considering we spend most of our downtime in front of the telly, I am starting to feel seriously short-changed.

How can I get my wife to up the ante when it comes to our box-set binge sessions, or at least show some appreciation for my world-class suggestions?

Ross, 38 – Manchester

Abbey: In any relationship it is crucial to have your own interests and hobbies, but when it comes to sitting down on an evening to watch television, you have to be on the same page and find some common ground. The good thing about our relationship is that Peter actually really enjoys watching the Kardashians.

Peter: I am a long sufferer when it comes to this problem, Ross. I do bite the bullet sometimes and begrudgingly watch *Grey's Anatomy* or the Kardashians, and I have even been known to get hooked myself. It rarely works the other way, though. If I want to watch a new Newcastle United documentary, I'd like to say Abbey lets me ... but she doesn't. I end up having to watch it in the back of the car when I am travelling for work instead.

Abbey: It's important to find something you can agree on, though, because I think if you are sitting in different rooms watching different things on an evening, that's surely the beginning of the end.

Peter: I don't know where things went wrong so that settling down to a box set at night has become the most exciting part of going to bed, but that's the reality we find ourselves in, so finding a good box set to enjoy together is crucial to a relationship. Finding one can be hard work, though. The scrolling on Netflix or Amazon is hellish. I've spent hours of my life just endlessly trying to find something.

Abbey: That's the one thing the algorithm hasn't quite cracked. There should be a special category available on the streaming services with programmes that suit couples.

Peter: Ultimately, though, Ross, I'm with you on this. You aren't getting enough credit for introducing your other half to what I see as being some of the best box sets ever written. *Peaky Blinders* and *The Sopranos* are classics. You're leading her to greatness and she can't see it, so maybe you're better off without her? Someone else will cherish you.

E

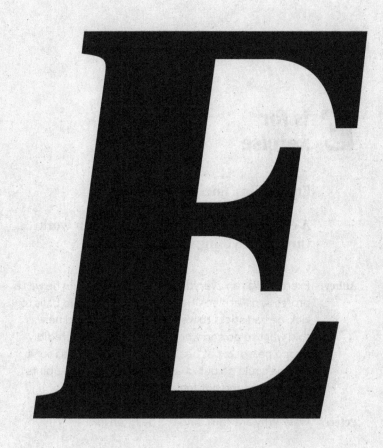

E *is for xercise*

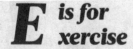

Endorphins. Energy. Exercise.

A couple that works out together can work through anything together, right?

Abbey: Exercise was an everyday thing for Pete when he was a professional athlete. He had a routine, he had balls to kick, he had sticks to weave in and out of, and he was told what to do and when to do it. He was incredibly fit and he worked at peak performance. He was so fit that he could go out of an evening, drink three pints of Guinness and not feel a thing the next day.

Peter: Was? Why are you using the past tense?

Abbey: I have a very fast metabolism, so I've never had to work out to keep the weight off. For me, exercise is about feeling good. It gives me energy and, as a mum of four, I'm always short of that. I often have a session on a Monday just to let off steam after a really busy weekend with the family. I really go for it, but then sometimes I don't work out for ages. It's a case of all or nothing with me.

Peter: We thought, when I retired, that a good way to exercise would be going on long dog walks together. Part of the pleasure of a dog walk is escaping the madness of the house and finding a little peace and quiet and companionship. But when Abs comes with me, it's an action replay of her behaviour when I'm watching football and she sits next to me jabbering away on the phone. We don't talk to each other for the whole walk. We don't spend quality time together. She'll just call her friend Caz and gossip endlessly about what she's going to wear on Saturday night.

Abbey: Not quite endlessly. I will hang up when we get to the part of the walk where the horses are. I'll say goodbye to Caz, play with the horses for a bit and then find another friend to call.

Peter: It's not relaxing in the slightest, which is why I no longer invite Abbey on dog walks.

Abbey: I also imagined that when Pete retired we would go to the gym together every day, but it's been the complete opposite. Pete is busier than ever, leaving me to my own devices when it comes to exercise. I'm a huge horse lover, so now that the kids are all in school I've taken the opportunity to get back in the saddle, and I've even tried to enthuse Pete. One of my lifelong ambitions was always to ride a horse along the beach. We did that together and both enjoyed it so much that we decided to take a horse ride up a mountain. The guy in charge was a cowboy in the best sense of the word, so impressively in control of our Spanish horses. He spoke no English, but we communicated through our love of the animals and even did some dressage together as we followed the trail up the mountain.

Dressage, unfortunately, was not in Pete's skill set. And you know what they say about horses' ability to detect a nervous rider. His decided to make a kamikaze run ...

Peter: Abbey was so taken with her Don Juan on horseback that she couldn't do anything about my horse suddenly bolting. I was holding on to it's neck, my feet dragging along the floor, tears in my eyes as it plunged towards a cliff. I thought I was goner.

Fortunately the cowboy managed to lasso me off the horse – impressive, to be fair – but the experience didn't fill me with a great passion for life in the saddle. I've only ever been thrown off or bolted.

It was more successful, I think, when I tried to get Abbey involved in a form of exercise that I love. No prizes for guessing what that was. We came across a beautiful golf course in Mexico that I couldn't not play. I dragged Abbey along as my caddy. I think it was quite up her street: driving the buggy and sunbathing with a cold bottle of beer while I hit a few balls. I think, in that moment, she really started to understand the attraction of golf as a pursuit.

Abbey: It *was* fun, until the buggy broke down and you made me carry your golf bag around for four hours.

Peter: You loved it.

Abbey: I really didn't love it. Give me a hunky cowboy on horseback any day.

Peter: I have a weird attitude towards exercise now. It was my job for 20-odd years, so it does feel like work still. I find it quite difficult to do it on my own. My fitness was always taken care of. I didn't have to think about it, because it was scheduled in for me. I just turned up and did what I was told to do. When you are a professional footballer you have very little control over even the most everyday tasks in your own life. It's like being in the army, I suppose: food, rations, manoeuvres – it's all organised for you. I do still go to the gym, but I miss being super-fit and the high you feel after playing a game. That's one hell of an endorphin rush.

Abbey: Every man wants to beat Pete at sport. At school sports day, all the fathers line up for the dads' race and you can see it on their faces: they're desperate to thrash him. It's a testosterone thing, I think. You wouldn't get women doing that. If there were a professional athlete in the mums' race, all the other women would just stand back in awe and cheer her on: 'You go for it, girl!'

A couple of years ago one dad turned up in spikes. He stood next to Pete. He eyed him up and down. He pawed the ground and beat his chest like an alpha silverback. Or something like that. When the race started, he tore past Pete and beat him. It was amazing. Nobody normally *does* manage to beat Pete, but on this occasion 'Fast Dad', as we call him, left him for dust.

Peter: I miss winning. Winning really matters to me. I miss competing at the highest level, and nothing can really replace it, but I do try to bring a bit of that competitive spirit when I play golf or tennis. I'm a terribly sore loser. If I don't win, I'll be in a mood for the rest of the day. It physically hurts me in the chest and puts me in a grump that I can't shift.

Abbey: I was the eldest of four, so I spent my childhood giving in to the babies and letting them win. Also, my dad was very old-school: he would take my brothers to football and all kinds of sports, but believed girls should be with their mum cooking, cleaning and shopping. So I have zero interest in winning for myself.

My children, though? Different matter. I'm afraid I'm a bit embarrassing. I get so into it when I'm cheering them on. Pete's the opposite. He felt quite a bit of pressure to succeed as a child, so he's really laid-back with our children – to the point of being horizontal. It's me who's on the touchline, shouting and screaming and running up and down.

Sophia is a strong swimmer. When she used to swim competitively I was a poolside maniac. I shouted myself hoarse! Poor Sophia had to sit in the back of the car listening to me trying to psyche her up before she went to a swimming meet. I'd be playing Eminem at full volume, singing 'Lose Yourself'. 'What are you?' I'd shout as she stared witheringly at me over the back seat, arms folded, mouth tightly shut. 'Are you a champ? Are you a swim warrior? You're a champ! Shout it back at me – I'm a champ! *I'm a champ!*'

Eventually she'd give in and agree that, yes, she was a champ, she was a swim warrior, just so I would let her out of the car. Only for me to end up poolside, running up and down, pumping the air with my fist, screaming her on.

As for me, when it comes to exercise and wellbeing, I'm one for a fad. Whatever the latest yoga moves or pilates techniques, count me in. 12 weeks of celery juice to improve our gut bacteria? Bring it on. Deep-meditation audio sleep guides? Been there, done that. Next on the list for me was a health-giving ice bath. What better way for us to support each other as a couple? Submerging oneself into an ice bath is difficult. I figured we could cheer each other on and get healthy together.

We managed it a few times, but then Pete started to complain.

Peter: I've done ice baths my whole professional career. I've done enough ice baths to last me lifetime. The thought of getting into another one was too much.

Abbey: So then I was on my own. I went to the ice bath one day, ready to refresh my body and sharpen my mind. I opened it up, expecting to see beautiful, fragile shards of ice coating the surface. What I actually saw was about two hundred bottles of Corona.

Peter: Genius, no? We were having a barbecue the next day and let's be honest: there's nothing worse than a warm lager on a hot afternoon. I didn't realise that Abbey planned to channel her inner Wim Hof that day, and I thought it was a spectacularly good idea for the ice bath to double as a booze refrigeration unit.

Obviously it was swiftly made clear to me that this was not a good idea at all. It was, in fact, a Very Bad Idea.

Abbey: If we lived in a frat house, it would be a brilliant idea. But we don't live in a frat house. We live in a family home and the ice bath is there for our health and wellbeing, not for Pete to chill his beers.

F

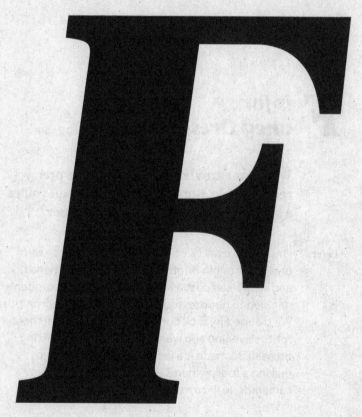

F *is for* *ancy Dress*

When you are six-foot-seven you're pretty recognisable. But what happens when you're a six-foot-seven Wookiee in the corner?

Peter: I'm quite partial to a bit of fancy dress. I once went on a night out in Brighton with a group of friends, and we walked past a fancy-dress shop. We suddenly decided to get dressed up. It was all very impromptu. We trooped in, took our clothes off, left them there for the evening and went out on the tiles. Getting dressed up made it a lot more fun. People enjoy making a fool of themselves in fancy dress. There's camaraderie in costumes.

My favourite outfits have been a headless horseman and Chewbacca. I make a great Chewbacca because I'm so tall. And, in fact, I think maybe that is part of what I love about dressing up. I'm pretty noticeable, thanks to my height. Dressed in jeans and a shirt, I stick out like a sore thumb, but somehow nobody notices me when I'm dressed as the giant Wookiee in the corner. Nobody bothers me. They've no idea who's inside the suit and my height isn't the most interesting thing about me. The most interesting thing about me is that I'm dressed as a big hairy monster.

I quite like a stag do. I'm used to hanging out with a gang of lads together. I can do the banter and the beer – it's second nature after being a footballer – and there's almost always fancy dress involved in stag weekends. On one particular do there were 30 grown men in fancy dress. Some wore wigs, others wore Stetsons, some were dressed as pirates, one bloke had a full-on cockerel outfit. The groom was dressed as a cow. He had an incredible black and white costume with a giant pink nose and huge udders hanging down. He'd also made a few adjustments of his own, such as cutting off one teat and putting his penis through. Like you do. We thought it was absolutely hilarious that he was walking around, jangling his udders with his old chap hanging out, but God knows what anyone else thought. With the benefit of hindsight, I'm just praying nobody noticed!

Abbey: We have a props box at home. I'd call it a dressing-up box, but that would be weird for grown-ups. So a props box it is, full of theatrical outfits that we can put on when we have people round and we've all had too much to drink. I might slip out of the room to get some more wine and come back in wearing something else. Elton glasses, anyone? An ABBA pantsuit ...?

Peter: A milkmaid's outfit?

Abbey: Dream on, babe.

F is for etishes

Oh Christ ... are we really doing this?

Peter: I'm here to tell you that Abbey has a thing about Vikings. Ooh, she loves a big, muscly Viking. Not totally sure why. The hairy legs and sandals? She gets enough of that at home. So maybe it's the shield and the horny hat. I keep thinking I might get myself a Viking outfit, just to spice things up a little, but I have a sneaking suspicion I'll end up looking like Rodney from that episode of *Only Fools and Horses* when he dresses up as a gladiator. And I don't think that's what she has in mind at all.

Abbey: That's quite enough about Vikings. Let's talk about Pete's mac fetish. And spoiler alert: we're not talking laptops.

Peter: Abbey collected me from training once dressed only in a mac with lacy underwear underneath. I've never forgotten it. Blew my mind. I've never seen anything like it ...

Abbey: And all of a sudden I think we might be getting to the bottom of Pete's trip to Burberry three Christmases in a row.

Peter: The mystery is solved.

F is for Floor Bed

A footballer, a model: young and free, no kids in tow, the world at their feet. You'd think their happiest times would be crazy nights out, hedonism and partying.

Think again.

Abbey: When I first moved in with Peter, the floor bed was our happy place. We would drag all the duvets, all the blankets, all the pillows and cushions on to the floor in front of the TV and just ... chill.

Peter: I'd train hard in the morning, then go to the gym followed by a big lunch so that I could refuel. By the time I got home I was so knackered that all I wanted to do was crash out in front of *The Sopranos*. The floor bed was a dream. When we look back, we remember those times spent on the floor bed, just being with each other, as some of the best of our lives.

Abbey: We often think of that floor bed. It's a reminder of what's important. When things get busy, and the time you have for each other gets eaten up by careers and kids and the mundane business of the everyday, then what really matters in a relationship are those moments spent together in quiet and comfort. With maybe a little jig to *The Sopranos* theme tune each time it comes on. (And no, before you ask, it wasn't our bonkbeat.)

Peter: Floor bed. Happy days. Strong recommend.

F is for ootball

Peter's take on football has been pretty well-documented. But what about Abbey? Does she share Peter's passion for the beautiful game?

Er, not really ...

Abbey: I've never been fazed by the whole football thing. Quite the opposite. My younger brother Sean was a footballer. From the age of eight he played for Liverpool and Everton, and he was one of the youngest ever players for Blackpool's first team. So my overwhelming childhood memory is of being dragged to boring football games in the cold and wet, sitting in the rain while watching my brother run around in the mud, then getting car sick while listening to the interminable football results on the radio on the way home. So even now, when I hear the football results on the telly, I want to be sick. The sound of someone announcing 'Newcastle 2, Burnley 1' is enough to make me want to chunder.

Peter: I watch a lot of football, for purely professional reasons, of course. You can't be a pundit without doing your research. It might *look* as if I'm parked with my arse on the sofa watching the game, but actually I'm working super-hard. It's very cerebral. Abbey, though, doesn't understand the Zen focus required. She has a habit of loitering in the background, chatting to her friends on speakerphone, which – not going to lie – makes it hard to concentrate on my studies. She also hasn't quite got her head round the fact that pausing a live game in order to nip out and get a takeaway really isn't the done thing. I mean, who would even *think* of doing that?

Abbey's *laissez-faire* attitude to match day was the same even when I was playing. She had a habit of phoning me at five to three on a Saturday afternoon to ask why I hadn't been in touch, and I'd have to explain that I was about to walk out on to the pitch in front of 70,000 fans to play Manchester United, and could we maybe chat a bit later. And often my phone would be connected to the speaker in the dressing room, spitting out some tunes so the lads could all get pumped up before the game. So when Abbey inevitably called three minutes before kick-off, it kind of killed the mood.

Abbey: Sorry not sorry. Truth is, football leaves me kind of cold. When Peter was playing for Liverpool, I used to give my tickets away to family members who were more interested in watching the game than I was. I did manage to make it to the game where Peter scored his first hat-trick, but I missed most of the excitement because I nipped out of the stands early so I could be first to the buffet. What can I tell you? A girl's got to eat.

Peter: A girl *has* got to eat. But a girl doesn't necessarily have to hand out a boy's prized England football shirts as tips for gardeners and delivery men. I don't *think* she'd go so far as to make the postman a gift of my Champions League medals, but I wouldn't bet my house on it.

Truth to tell, however, there's something refreshing about Abbey's attitude towards the game. There are some footballers' wives – naming no names – who'd give their husbands a full-on analysis of the game when they got home. *I can't believe you missed that penalty. You should have kicked the ball like this, not like that ...*

Abbey was the absolute opposite. I'd come home and nine times out of ten she'd talk about anything but football. And when she *did* talk about football, she had her own unique spin on it. *You hit the bar? That's much more impressive than scoring a goal because the bar's much smaller ...*

Which, I have to say, strangely made me feel better for missing a sitter from three yards. So thanks, babe!

F is for friends

Men like doing things with their friends: golf, watching football, having a beer. Women just talk to their friends. All. The. Time.

Abbey: Each time Pete signed to a different club, we had to move, sometimes to the opposite end of the country. We'd find ourselves in a completely new city that I'd never even visited before, let alone had friends to hang out with. It's hard to keep making new friends all the time, so I've tended to stick with the same girls who have been with me for ever. I love my friends so much that I even named one of my children after my close friend Liberty. They mean the world to me. I don't get to spend lots of time with them, but that doesn't stop us keeping in touch. I speak to my best friend Caz ten times a day. She knows everything about my life because she practically gets a live running commentary.

Friends play a huge role in our life. There's nothing better for us than going to a festival or on holiday with a big group. They're all great characters who have been with us from the beginning.

Peter: Trouble is, Abbey wants us to do romantic things as a couple all the time, but can't help herself inviting twenty people along at the same time.

Abbey: That's because when it's just the two of us, I get boring Pete. We'll go away and he'll announce that he's not drinking because he wants to get healthy on this trip. We'll decide to watch a movie and he'll start snoring after a few seconds. I'll want to chat and he'll pick up a book! If our friends are with us, though, I know I'll get fun Pete and I know he'll be on fire! I like to be entertained and our friends are all big characters, believe it or not, I'm one of the quietest in the group. My friends are all nutty and hilarious ...

Peter: ... and they *talk*. I went to pick Abbey up from a ladies-who-lunch type of affair, and when I walked into the room I saw a bunch of women all talking at the same time, and yet all apparently listening to each other's conversation. It was insane.

Abbey: It's a female thing. We can multitask.

Peter: I have my friends from school still, but I just don't get to see them much anymore. We do speak quite a lot on the phone. Well, when I say 'speak', what I mean is that we WhatsApp each other. Women pick up the phone for anything. Abbey calls me about 15 times a day, and that's just when I'm in the house. But if my phone ever rings and it's not Abbey, I panic. I think, *Oh my God, someone's died!* I feel like people only really call me if there is something serious to say. I like to know what it is before I answer, because the thought of being caught off guard worries me. So, often, if my phone goes and it's a number I don't know, I just won't answer it.

Maintaining a network of friends is quite hard. You've got to look after them and be nice to them and see them, but when you've all got your own families and jobs, life gets in the way. It doesn't help that we're very last-minute people. Everything in our life is very organised except our social life, so when we do have a window, we grab it. Our friends, though, always seem to be booked up for months. The first sunny weekend of the summer hits, and we'll say, 'Do you want to come round for a barbecue tomorrow?' But they won't have a free weekend until mid-November.

Abbey: We love having friends round, though. We love celebrating kids' birthdays together and holidaying as a group. I'm super proud to call my friends my friends, and I think people envy our friendship group. They see us acting silly, causing a scene, having so much fun. People come up to us when we're out in public and comment on how we must have the best friendship group.

Peter: Apart from that time when I joined a group next to ours who were playing a drinking game I'd never played before. Abbey couldn't understand why I spent the whole night with a bunch of randoms on the other side of the room. Hard truth: that was a better friendship group than ours.

Abbey: Pete doesn't hang around with many footballers, with one exception: Glen Johnson. I sometimes think he'd prefer to be married to Glen than to me. Glen wouldn't mind if Pete came home late from golf or was shit at DIY. It'd be a match made in heaven.

Agony ~~Aunt~~ Ab

Dear Abbey,

There's a new Spanish hunk in the office and he's hot property. He's like a sexy matador in a herd of horny cows.

One lunchtime we got chatting. He let slip that the way to his heart was through his stomach and sushi was his favourite food. Like a lovesick idiot, I told him it also happened to be my signature dish and that I'd bring some in for him. I hoped it would help me stand out from the crowd, and that if I did something thoughtful he might ask me out on a date.

I can't cook at all, though. I could burn an ice cube. That's how bad I am.

So I found the best sushi in the area and spent a complete bomb there. I carefully packed it all in

Tupperware to cover my tracks. One of the girls in the office even caught me, and I had to bribe her with tea and biscuits so she didn't say anything.

It was all worth it, though. We sat together laughing and flirting for the entire lunch break. It was one of the best first dates I've ever had – and we were at work.

When he texted me later that night, though, he said I'd given him food poisoning and it was coming out at both ends. I couldn't believe it. I just don't do shellfish, so I'd steered clear of the crab.

We had an important company trip planned to meet a new client, and he had to miss the entire thing because he was too sick. I felt so guilty that I stepped into his position and picked up the extra work – I didn't want my stupid antics to cause any more trouble.

When we got back the boss pulled me aside to congratulate me on nailing the pitch and said that the client wanted me on the job!

Now the Spanish hunk hates me and thinks I did the whole thing on purpose, that I stole his job and used it to get a promotion.

How do I clear my name and get back into his good books? I still really fancy him and if I hadn't accidentally poisoned him I think we'd be great together ...

Anne, 28 – London

Peter: Honesty is always the best policy, and everything here spiralled from a lie. Surely he was always going to find out that Anne couldn't make sushi, even if it had all gone more smoothly and they ended up together.

Abbey: Starting off any relationship by being deceitful and disguising the person you really are is never going to turn out well.

Peter: Maybe if Anne were to come clean he would see the funny side, and it would be one of those things they laugh about in years to come. There's something very endearing about someone trying to do something so nice and it all backfiring and becoming a failure. She meant well when she tried to impress him and, putting myself in his position, if someone went to the lengths that Anne did to impress me it would warm my heart.

Abbey: Isn't it still a red flag that someone is willing to lie, even if they mean well by it?

Peter: If you'd said to me, 'I really like men who can decorate,'

I would have said I could and then given it a try. When you came around I'd have just been doing a bit of impromptu painting of the walls.

Abbey: That's not true. I do say I like a man who can cook or build stuff, and you never do either.

Peter: That's different – we're past that.

Abbey: Lying about the sushi may have been the catalyst for this situation, but what about the issue of the job? Everything's pointing towards sabotage in his eyes. It looks like she's given him food poisoning to steal his job, and even though she didn't, if she liked him that much she shouldn't have taken over the job. It's like *The Devil Wears Prada*. You shouldn't be jumping into someone else's shoes as soon as you know they're not fit to do the job, especially if you like them.

Peter: But fellas come and go, and this job only comes around once. There'll be other Spanish hunks, Anne. Move on!

G

G is for Girl Talk

It's a man's world, professional male football. Sure, Becks might sport the occasional sarong, but who could be more macho and virile than a guy who spent his formative years in Premier League changing rooms?

Sorry to disappoint. It turns out that Abbey's girl talk is having a surprising effect on Peter ...

Abbey: We've spent so much time together, me and Pete, that he's basically turned from a husband to a dad, to a gay best friend, to a full-on gossip-loving, face-cream-wearing, scented-bath fanatic. In short, he's turning into a girl. It's happened by stealth. Just like the endless football trivia I'm exposed to seeps into my brain to the point that I find myself able to hold my own in a conversation about Adebayor's transfer from Arsenal to Man City (yawn), so Peter's background knowledge of my friends' lives, loves and outfit choices has started to have a dramatic effect on his personality.

Peter: No point me denying it.

Abbey: It happened gradually, and the first indications were slight. We were lying in bed and Peter suddenly said, 'Did Caz end up finding a dress for her fiftieth?' Now, don't let me bore you with the saga of Caz's birthday dress. Suffice to say that it had gone on for several months. But I'd assumed any talk of it had gone over Peter's head. If he can't remember to pack the kids' PE kit, surely he'd never remember the minutiae of Caz's sartorial dilemmas.

Apparently not. Apparently the girl talk had wormed its way into his consciousness.

Not long after that, we're discussing a male actor in a movie. I ask, 'What do you think of him?'

I fully expect a non-committal shrug. What I don't expect is for Peter to say, 'Not really my type. I don't like that greasy look on men.'

Peter: Frankly, I was as surprised as Abbey when that comment popped out of my mouth. I couldn't quite believe what I'd just said. It was like Abbey's girl talk was taking me over. I felt like I'd become one of her friends.

Abbey: Even more so when I pointed out a dress and Peter said, 'That would look lovely with an oversized clutch bag.'

Peter: An oversized clutch bag?! What am I becoming?

Abbey: I have a huge array of lotions and potions for my skin, and essential oils for the bath. Now Peter's all over them. He creeps craftily up to bed 15 minutes early, dumps a whole bottle of essential oils in his bath and slathers his face in cream. I've had to start hiding all my skincare products from him.

Peter: Not a problem. I went online and bought myself a big box of Elemis Pro-Collagen Marine Cream. My favourite. Improves skin firmness and elasticity, increases hydration levels, transforms your complexion ... Now we have endless deliveries of beauty products. Lip balms. Factor 50. Hair salt spray for volume and texture. Because I'm worth it.

G is for Golf

Footballers and golf go together like gin and tonic or sausages and mash. But what is the attraction of a day spent on the course? Could it possibly be the revelries that follow?

Peter: If you walked into my house and spent 20 minutes in my shoes, you'd immediately understand the appeal of golf. There are a million people here all the time. There might be workmen, builders and kids (many of them mine). There might be dogs, cats, ducks and sheep. It's chaotic and noisy. It's bedlam. Compare that to the prospect of playing golf in the middle of nowhere, under the clear blue sky, amid the peace of the green and the trees. Give me a chance to spend four and half hours with my friends on the quiet of the golf course and I am there.

And why do footballers specifically play golf? Well, we have time, for a start, especially if we don't actually play football anymore! It's also a form of exercise that's not too physically exerting. Footballers aren't allowed to ski, and you can't play tennis, as you really don't want to injure yourself by pulling a muscle or tearing a ligament. Golf is a good way of doing something with your mates that won't lead to a career-ruining night in A&E. It's exercise without injury. I used to see it as an old man's sport, but now I don't mind coming across as an old man for liking it. Then, of course, there's the bit that comes after. The après-golf, if you like ...

Abbey: When Pete's finished at the golf course, he likes to bring all the men back to the house. They crawl through the door on their hands and knees, as they've been at the bar so bloody long. I stand there with my face mask on, watching them pitifully stagger past me on their way towards the sofa for more drinks.

Peter: Abbey has a special golf face – stern, disapproving, one eyebrow raised – but I know she's secretly delighted when the boys come over. She'd much rather we were fooling around at our house than have me conked out on my mate's sofa.

And, to a certain extent, she's one of the boys. She's good with the banter and the beers. If there's a big match on, she loves to join in the tension – the penalties and all that. The lads love her too, but it's the kind of love that goes hand in hand with also being absolutely shit-scared of her. As you may have noticed, Abbey doesn't mince her words. She calls a spade a spade, she's funny and sharp and has a sarcastic wit, but if you mess with her house or muck up her furniture, you'll sure as hell know about it.

Unfortunately, if you've indulged in a spot of après-golf, the chances of house-messing and furniture-mucking-up are relatively high ...

Abbey: Pete brought four mates home the other night after golf. When they arrived, not one of them could stand. They'd been drinking all day. They crawled in through the front door, and since I didn't know them that well, I thought I'd kindly let them use the nice glasses we bought in Portugal. They smashed them. Every. Single. One. When I woke up there was a whole bottle of white wine tipped up over the marble worktop in the kitchen, its contents dripping on to the floor. Thank God it was white and not red. But even so – are they ever coming back here again?

Absolutely not.

H

H is for angovers

We've all been there, right? The cracking headache, the horrible nausea, the nasty suspicion that you might just want to die. And the parents among us will know the abject horror of hearing the patter of tiny feet outside the bedroom door the morning after the night before.

But what if we've got hangovers all wrong? What if they need a rebrand?

Abbey: Let's get one thing straight: a hangover when you have to look after kids is the worst kind of hell. Life doesn't stop just because Mum and Dad had a glass of wine too many. The kids are up at six in the morning no matter if your head feels like someone hit it with an axe. The swimming lessons and play dates don't let up just because you want to curl up and die, and bedtime can't come soon enough. If you're parenting on a hangover, you have our undying sympathy.

But we're here to tell you that hangovers don't have to be that way. Properly handled, hangovers can be a catalyst for the most perfect day imaginable.

Peter: I'm a recent convert to the hangover. Its pleasures are new to me. When I was playing football I didn't drink loads, but we'd sometimes go out for a few beers after a game. I didn't suffer at all the morning after, probably because I was so fit at the time. I never really understood why people seemed to feel the urge to lie in bed all day, but I did have an inkling that hangovers might not be as fearsome as their reputation suggested when I saw how Abbey and our friends Jason and Stacey dealt with them.

Abbey: We'd go out as a foursome on a Saturday night when Peter was playing for Liverpool. Peter would always have to get up for training on a Sunday – fit as a fiddle, bright as a daisy – leaving me, Jason and Stacey to nurse our aching heads. I'd get into bed with them and we'd spend the day watching *Hollyoaks* repeats and occasionally kicking Jason out to make us tea and toast. When Pete got back, he'd bring us McDonald's or a roast dinner takeaway. And those lovely, lazy hangover days were just perfect.

Peter: It took me a while to see the attraction. Only when I stopped playing and got a bit older did I even start to get hangovers. And gradually I started to come round to Abbey's point of view that, properly handled, a hangover is a thing of beauty, something to revel in and enjoy.

Abbey: The best time for a hangover as a couple is when you're away by yourselves for a couple of days. No kids, no pressure, you can just lie in bed all day, call room service and revel in your misery. We recently went to a three-day birthday party at a hotel and we were feeling a bit nervous – it was a thirtieth, so everyone was going to be a bit younger than us. We managed to stay up with the cool kids until three in the morning and woke up the next day predictably woolly-headed. So we didn't move from the room. We ordered half the room-service menu, went back to sleep, had a massage and then ordered the other half of the room-service menu. Macaroni cheese, pizza, cheese soufflé, deep-fried camembert. The works. We watched some movies. We went to sleep again. It was pretty much the most perfect day we'd spent for years. Without the hangover, we'd have been up and doing things, but let's face it: the day wouldn't have been half so memorable.

Peter: So here's to hangovers. Properly handled and lovingly shared, they're one of life's great pleasures.

H is for Honeymoons

Your honeymoon. The most romantic holiday of your life. Just do your best not to commit your wife to a watery grave in the process.

Peter: We made a total mess of our honeymoon. We'd just had a baby, so we didn't want to fly far. We went to Ibiza, not for the clubbing, but to a spa hotel on a cliff in the north of the island. It looked perfect: luxurious, indulgent and relaxing, and we couldn't wait to be pampered: a real treat for any exhausted new parent.

Right from the beginning we realised that this wasn't going to be the break we had dreamed of. There weren't enough loungers by the pool, so we ended up sitting on two uncomfortable upright chairs, side by side in the shade, without so much as a sniff of our long-promised welcome Bellini.

Abbey: When we went for lunch I wanted a nice bit of fresh fish with some salad, and Pete wanted paella. As we placed our order, the waiter shook his head. Paella was a dish intended for two. Pete didn't mind – he was happy to pay for the double portion, and he'd probably have eaten the lot anyway. The waiter was having none of it. He wagged his finger and shook his head. Paella was a dish for two and Pete was only one! We reassured them that we were happy to pay, but they refused and in the end they wouldn't serve us at all! So that was a lovely honeymoon lunch.

We went back to sit with our feet in the pool, already feeling pretty glum, when a seagull flew over and shat on Pete's leg.

It was at that point that we decided to leave.

Showing off his romantic side, Pete hired a private boat to take us to Mallorca. We'd be picked up near the cliff-top hotel and we'd sail on our own, leaving all the stress of the start of our honeymoon behind us. I pictured myself leaning back, my hair blowing in the cool sea breeze, the sun shining on my face, a sense of calm and contentment washing over me.

Unfortunately, we didn't bank on it being one of the choppiest passages of open water in the world.

It started out like something from a movie. Dolphins were following our boat, leaping into the air before throwing themselves back into the crystal-clear water. But then the wind picked up. Waves started flying over the side of the boat. The crew were vomiting.

The waitress who was supposed to be pouring the champagne was horizontal on the bench next to me, looking a pale shade of green, clutching her sick bag and telling us that we might capsize. I thought I was going to die.

Peter: Meanwhile, I'm with the captain, who was barely able to hold on to the wheel as we lurched from side to side, waves pouring over the side of the boat. I smiled at him and said, 'We're going to get through this OK, aren't we?'

I was expecting an encouraging response from our jovial Spanish skipper. Something like, 'We get this weather all the time. It's no problem.' But no. He looked me dead in the eye and, with terror written all over his face, said, 'I am not so sure.'

Which is exactly what you don't want to hear in the middle of a storm, miles from land, with your new wife being spun around below deck like she's in a washing machine. I went down below to check on Abbey, and I just smiled and waved. I think I even gave her a big thumbs up. I hoped she couldn't tell how scared I was. It was like the boat scene from *The Wolf of Wall Street*.

Finally, we arrived in Mallorca. I'd planned a big romantic gesture, where I would theatrically present Abbey with a stunning diamond bracelet but the one I ended up giving her wasn't quite befitting of such a grand gesture. When I handed Abbey a small brown paper envelope instead of that iconic turquoise box, her face said it all. We had our first marital row right there and then, and I was so fed up I hurled the bracelet into the sea.

What a great honeymoon! I'd been dissed by the waiter, shat on by a seagull, nearly killed my wife, had an epic row and thrown a fistful of diamonds into the sea! They're probably still there, if you want to go and find them.

H is for Hotels

Hotels. A home from home. A big comfy bed and someone else to cook and clean for you. Perfect, right?

Well, possibly not ...

Peter: You'd think that when we manage a night away from the kids in a hotel, we'd have a long sleep, a leisurely lie-in and a room-service binge. And sometimes we do (see H is for Hangover). But unless it's a matter of dire medical (OK, self-inflicted) necessity, we keep our distance from that room-service tray. After a lifetime of being locked up in hotel rooms before playing in important away games, I can't bear eating in the bedroom. Dinner off a tray is my idea of hell. Call me picky, but I like to eat at a proper table in a proper dining room. Why would you want to fall asleep next to the remnants of your last meal? Why would you want to wake up with cold chips six inches from your face? It makes me feel a little unwell just thinking about it.

Abbey: Hangovers aside, I don't want my food brought to me because I prefer to smash the hotel breakfast. A buffet breakfast is my favourite thing in the world. I go to bed dreaming of it if I'm away, and if I make it down to the breakfast room to find nothing but a disappointing plate of cheese and ham, I get angry. That's an amateur-hour hotel breakfast, in my opinion.

I want a choice of everything. The full monty. Eggs, cake, pastries, cooked breakfast, waffles, cereal, yoghurt, juice. I have no embarrassment about loading up my tray. I pretend I'm getting food for the rest of the family, when really it's all for me. I'm a buffet-returner, too. I have no qualms about that. I'll go back for the pastries, the croissants, the pains au chocolat. I don't consider myself done until I've eaten at least three separate courses. Three whole platefuls, from fruit through to cake. I don't care what anyone thinks – I'll sit there for hours, working my way through the whole lot.

Peter: However, even with a fabulous buffet, hotels are not all they're cracked up to be. Sometimes staying with the kids in a hotel is more work than being at home. We tend to get interconnecting rooms, with the girls sleeping in one room and the rest of us in the other. Sometimes Abbey ends up in a room with the two girls, and then I'll be in the other room with the two boys – one in my bed, one in a cot in the bathroom because there's no floor space in the room. You can imagine the ninja tactics required for a stealthy midnight wee. You can't turn the light on in the bathroom in case you wake the baby, and the room echoes and magnifies the merry tinkle of pee on porcelain. Not an easy way to answer an urgent call of nature.

Abbey: I suppose it's a bit better than a friend of mine who spent the whole of a holiday asleep in the bath so she and her son could seek refuge from her husband's snores. The fan didn't work when the lights were off, so the room became hotter and hotter, and increasingly airless. I think she had it all wrong: in that situation, I would have relegated the husband to the bathroom.

Whatever the sleeping arrangements, this game of musical beds means Peter and I will have no physical contact for the entire duration of a family hotel trip. Which isn't quite how we tend to envisage our holiday time.

Peter: Wherever we stay, we end up leaving something behind. Last time we went on holiday, it was such chaos that we managed to leave all our iPads on the flight. You can imagine how distressing it was to be parted from our beloved electronic babysitters. But not even the iPads are as sacred as the items the children carry around with them for comfort. Johnny carries a super-king-size pillow wherever he goes, not a tiny little cushion more befitting of a five-year-old. It's bigger than he is. I've no idea how we found ourselves in a position where we have to carry 'Pio' halfway across the world, but we do. Pio even has to have a special White Company pillowcase with black trim. We should have shares in that shop because we've left spares in hotels and elsewhere all over the world.

Abbey: Then there's Jack's blanket: Blank. You can see what he did there. Blank has more airmiles than Father

Christmas. He's been left behind, rescued off beaches and packed into Jiffy bags to be posted across the world and reunited with us more times than we can count. Unlike Pio, who can be replaced, there is no back-up Blank. We've tried to find one. We've sourced the same style of blanket and cut off a little piece in the same shape, but Blank has received so much love and attention, and smells and feels so different to a new blanket, that he's completely irreplaceable. The other day, I was parking my car in London when I saw Blank in the passenger seat next to me. I panicked: what if someone stole the car? They could keep the car, I wouldn't care about that, but to lose Blank would be unthinkable. In the end I found myself sitting in a smart West End salon having my nails done with Blank on my knee, just so I knew it was safe.

Peter: So, with four children, Pio and Blank to keep safe, and with the high-level jeopardy of sneaking into the bathroom for a crafty wee, you can see why staying at home is sometimes more appealing than staying in even the plushest of hotels. All we'd really need is someone to serve us a cake course for breakfast.

I

I *is for* *ck*

We all have them, don't we? Those little habits or annoyances that we see in others and which make us cringe ...

Abbey: I always thought I didn't have many icks. I thought I was ickless. But then someone sent me a meme on Instagram. It showed a guy's earlobe flapping in the wind. That night I looked at Pete while he was sleeping and I saw the way his earlobe flopped down, and what can I say? It turned out I did have an ick after all.

In fact, the floppy earlobe opened the ick floodgates. It robbed me of my ick virginity. All of a sudden I found myself thinking of those little half-socks guys buy to wear with their trainers ...

Peter: Like the ones I wear for golf?

Abbey: Just like the ones you wear for golf. The idea of a man thinking, *I know, I'll buy a nice little sock that shows off my lovely little ankle* ... It's enough to make me shudder.

And *then* I found myself thinking of the way Pete talks to waiters abroad, loudly in broken English but with a clumsy foreign accent: *Escuse me, can we 'ave dos beers and a jambon pizza? You like ze football, no?*

And *then* I remember being in the car with Pete, looking up from my phone and watching him singing both verses to 'Candy Shop' by 50 Cent, giving it everything like he was actually on stage. Ick, anyone?

And then, of course, there's the ultimate ick. The ick to end all icks: men farting. As a rule, women don't fart in public, but men do and it just makes me want to die. It's the biggest turn-off on the planet. When I was growing up, my brother would just sit on the couch next to me and fart as loudly as he could. Traumatising. I can honestly say that in 17 years of being together, Pete has never farted in front of me unless it's been by accident.

Peter: I'm not sure that's true, but I wouldn't rub your face in it, literally or metaphorically. I'm a gentleman like that.

So it turns out Abbey's not immune to the ick, after all. On the other hand, I think I'm a bit more laid-back. For me, the biggest ick is the word 'ick' itself. It's a *horrible* word. Totally gives me the ... well, I won't say it, but it's up there in my list of worst words and phrases ever. Words and phrases guaranteed to put me on edge. Up there with phrases that seem to be all over Instagram and TikTok, like 'Gen Z', 'My bad' and, worst of all, 'Oh my days'. Maybe I'm just getting old, but the worst is when people from Surrey use that language, like they're from the rough end of Compton. Makes me shudder.

I think I can honestly say, though, that there's nothing about Abbey that gives me the ick. Her earlobes are perfect, her taste in socks immaculate and her wind is never broken. So no complaints there.

Abbey: Which is the correct answer ...

I is for the Ideal Home

Home is where the heart is. Or, for your average footballer, where the five-a-side football pitch with integrated cocktail bar is. So has Abbey's notion of the ideal home been unduly influenced by her exposure to the interior-design tastes of the Premier League?

Peter: Back in the day, the standard footballer's house was a huge mock-Tudor monstrosity with an in-and-out drive, a swimming pool out the back and a big dog in the driveway next to an oversized SUV. Then they all got replaced by enormous glass houses with swimming pools and gyms in the basement and games rooms out the back. There's always a kitchen full of cupboards that nobody knows how to open. There will certainly be a five-a-side football pitch in the garden – not for the children, but for the lads to play on after a few beers – and invariably a basketball hoop for everyone to pretend that they could have been Michael Jordan. Often there's a massive Bond-villain fish tank that lights up bright blue at night.

Abbey thinks I have terrible taste. Left to my own devices I'd probably still be playing PlayStation in my childhood bedroom. So I've quite rightly had absolutely nothing to do with how any of our houses have been decorated.

Abbey: I'm the absolute opposite. There's nowhere I'd rather be than at home. I love it when we're all together in our sacred space. During the pandemic, for all the terrible things happening around the world, we had the best time at home. We were really happy and content, just the six of us, spending all that time together in a home so calm and full of love.

So I take a huge amount of pride in everything looking beautiful. I always want the house to be clean and tidy, and I absolutely love making a house a home. The detail is so important to me.

Peter: It's a skill and an art, and I'm so grateful to Abbey for having made every home we've ever lived in totally beautiful.

Abbey: And there have been a lot of them. We used to have to move *all* the time because of Pete's football. With every transfer to a new club, we'd pack up and move on. Sometimes it would happen pretty much overnight. When he signed for Stoke, within two days of the call to say they were interested we had to move out of one house in Surrey and into another hundreds of miles away. Most people take years planning a long-distance move like that. Pete had me. He walked out of the door of one home and in through the door of another and, just like magic, everything was exactly as it should have been. Our stuff had been moved in and set up almost exactly as it was, albeit in an entirely different place.

Peter: Abbey was so organised. It was a bit like *Challenge Anneka*. I think she got a thrill out of achieving the impossible in such a short space of time.

Abbey: The surroundings are important, of course, but for me home is wherever Pete is. Some footballers' wives stay put when their husband joins a new club. I guess that works for them, and some families can't move at the drop of a hat like we did. The children might be in school with exams, and you can't just up and move them mid-term. But for me, it was always important that we stay together. The only exception was when Pete went to Burnley. We knew it was only for a short period and I was quite pregnant with Jack, so it didn't make sense for us all to move.

Peter: That time we spent apart helped me make the decision to retire. I was getting less and less time on the pitch, and it reached the point when I started to think, *What's the point of this? My family isn't around me, I'm lonely, I miss them and I'm spending most of the match with my arse on the bench.*

We bought a plot of land in Surrey and built our own house. It took two years and Abbey designed the whole lot.

Abbey: It's our first proper home of our own. We rented a lot when Pete was playing, so although I could furnish a place the way I wanted it, I could never do anything that permanently changed it. Now I had my chance to start from scratch. I'd always loved old houses with Victorian architecture and original features, so building something new was daunting. Worth it, though: I love how comfy, warm and welcoming our home feels, and it's all the more special for having been designed by us.

Interior design is my passion. I love going to antiques fairs and looking for vintage bits and bobs – you have to get up early in the morning to find the best items, so I go with my torch at the ready. And I love incorporating marble into our house, even though I'm also a clean freak, so it's a constant challenge to keep it from looking like it has been trashed. The first coffee ring on the marble was a traumatising moment for me, but with four kids, Jeffrey the dog and two cats, I just have to let it go. I still like things to be tidy, and clearing away the toys every evening is my own personal *Groundhog Day*. Put Pete in charge, though, and you'd think we'd been burgled every evening ...

Peter: My only bugbear about Abbey's approach to interior design is the cushions on the bed. There are approximately five thousand of them, and each night I have to battle my way into bed, throwing armfuls of cushions on to the floor, only to put them back on the bed in the morning. I just don't get it.

Abbey: One day, I want us to be in the proper countryside, surrounded by fields. I want to collect eggs from our own hens in the morning. I want to grow my own vegetables. I'd love the kids to be outdoors swinging on a rope, camping in the garden, riding horses or toasting marshmallows on a fire, not sitting there staring at their frigging iPads. That's the dream.

Peter: For Abbey, maybe. I like it where we are. I just want a peaceful time, a nice, quiet life in a comfortable house.

Abbey: Unfortunately, you gave up that right when you had four kids!

J

J is for Jealousy

We've all got a bit of the green-eyed monster in us ... haven't we?

Abbey: Hand on heart, I'm not a jealous person. I don't get envious of people. When good things happen to those I love, I couldn't be happier. I'm the first to call up and congratulate them. The green-eyed monster and I are not well-acquainted.

But ...

Being married to someone in the public eye means that everyone feels they know my husband and they all want a piece of him. I do find that very hard to take.

It was worse when we were younger. We'd go out to a bar and women would barge me out of the way to get close to Pete. They'd literally elbow me or shove me in the back. It was quite something. They'd laugh at his jokes, flick their hair seductively and pout. It was crazy. I was pretty insecure back then, and it did make me jealous.

But there comes a moment, especially after you've brought four children into the world together, that you have to let go of those feelings and be confident that nobody else matters.

Peter: It's hard to know who you can trust in situations like the one Abbey describes. Football clubs are always trying to get their players to settle down and marry the girl from school so you don't end up being taken for a ride and making truly terrible mistakes. It's hard, though, if you're a local boy made good who has come up through the ranks. You're the local celebrity, so everybody knows who you are when you're out on the town. Everyone wants their piece of you. It's like you have a target on your back. The managers give you all the right advice. *Don't go to the local clubs, don't drink too much, don't make a fool of yourself.* But show me an 18-year-old who wants to live their life like that, especially if they have a few quid in their pocket.

J is for obs

One of the secrets of a happy marriage is a fair division of labour. There are countless jobs involved in the successful running of a happy family, and it's important that neither partner feels in any way overworked or taken for granted. So if that's not the case, if there's a mismatch in that respect, it would be fair game for the therapy couch ...

Abbey: A mother's work is never done. Isn't that what they say? But what about a father's work? In our house, that should be easily completed because Pete only has three jobs. I do everything else.

Job number one: take out the bins.

Peter: Which I do every now and then. No problem there. Man's work. Sorted.

Abbey: Job number two: open the mail and go through it. Check for the important stuff. Make sure none of it slips under the radar. Unfortunately – or, for Pete, fortunately – we have the luxury of a PA. So Pete's diligence in mail-opening has lapsed somewhat. As far as I can tell, he just shoves it all into a bigger envelope and posts it off to our PA to deal with.

Job number three: the dog. None of that 'the front end is mine, the back end is yours' nonsense. Pete's job is to feed, walk and clean up after the dog.

Peter: Worth bearing in mind here that this is the dog I didn't want in the first place.

Abbey: Pete's three jobs are not onerous. They're not a big deal. But they do seem to mean that the job part of his brain is working at capacity, so if I ask him to do anything extra, there's normally some sort of overload and malfunction.

If I give him a shopping list, without fail he'll return with one item missing and two of everything else. It makes no sense. If he does the school run, I'll have all the kids' bags packed with military precision by the door for him to load into the boot. As sure as eggs is eggs, we'll get a phone call from the school a couple of hours later, saying one of the kids doesn't have their PE kit, which is still in the boot of the car. Cue another hour-and-ten round trip to drop it off.

Peter: Fair comment. That does happen a lot. In my defence, have you seen how many bags a kid has to take to school these days? You have to hang the games kit off them, like they're a walking coat rail. I can't even see the child when they're going in to school – they look like some kind of bag monster.

Abbey: I leave Pete very clear instructions about what to do, but he just can't follow them. If I ask him to supervise the kids' homework, I'll show him a note from the teacher: 'Liberty's work is very good but she needs to remember her capital letters and full stops.' You can bet your boots that by the time the homework's done under Pete's watchful eye, there won't be a single capital letter or full stop in sight.

Peter: What Abbey fails to understand is that there's only so many jobs a man can do in one day. There's a job upper limit. You can't do them all. It's just a fact of life, the way we're wired, a law of nature. Some of those jobs are just going to fall by the wayside. And the trouble is, it's the ones you *don't* do that get mentioned, not the ones you *do* do. So we can't win, and to be honest I think we deserve a little bit more sympathy ...

Agony ~~Aunt~~ Ab

Dear Abbey,

I have one mate who is the life of the party every time he comes out: he often does things that make our night. However, since he's got a girlfriend, she has completely taken over his life and he's no longer allowed to see his friends, as she doesn't like us. We've tried everything to get her involved in the group, even taking her out on her birthday, but nothing works. She didn't even say thank you. It affects all of us, but most of all it affects him. Last year she forced him to leave a festival early to be with her rather than us.

Have you got any suggestions on how we can get our mate out of the cage his girlfriend is keeping him in? We just want him back.

Eliot, 20 – Birmingham

Peter: Unfortunately this is something that you see regularly with friends. They do get girlfriends and like to spend time with them - it's basically a fact of life.

Abbey: It is a fact of life and it's part of growing up but I don't feel like it happened to us, you know. We're good as friends as well as in a relationship and we love being part of a group together. But there are people we know who have either got a boring girlfriend or a boring boyfriend - they're just not on the same page.

And that creates problems further down the line, especially in a group. If someone's personality changes around their new partner, I don't think they're fully compatible.

Peter: Exactly right. Eliot here is reaching out an olive branch to his mate's new girlfriend, he's inviting her to things and she's making no effort whatsoever. I think he should sabotage it.

Abbey: His friend was the life and soul of the party and now he's boring because he's doing what his girlfriend says. I just hate it when this happens in a relationship, so I agree.

Sabotage it. Get rid of her.

K

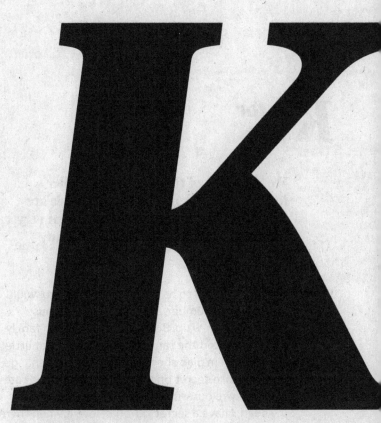

K is for kids

We have four of them – the 'footballer's four', like Beckham and Rooney. Kids are time-consuming, expensive and often very annoying. And we wouldn't have it any other way ...

Peter: I never expected to have four. I thought two would be the magic number, a boy and a girl, because that's how I grew up. But Abbey's from a big family and she wanted the same. So Abbey won that little battle, and I'm glad she did. Now I wouldn't change a thing. I take secret pride in how good our kids are when they're out with us. Is it bad to admit that, in my head, I have a secret kid-off? I love it when there's a family on the plane with just one child screaming their head off, while our four are quiet and well-behaved. It gives me a nice little moment of smug satisfaction.

For us, lockdown was a strangely precious time amid the wider misery. Time that we could all spend together. We said to each other at the time: if this was life for ever, we'd be happy.

Abbey: We brought all four kids up the same way, but each of them is completely different in character.

There's Sophia, the eldest. She's like Saffy from *Ab Fab*. Her room is immaculate, she has a whole skincare routine that takes an hour a day. She has the teenager attitude down to a tee. *Ugh, Mum, what are you wearing? You're the most uncool person on the planet*. We all need someone to keep our feet on the ground, don't we? Sophia's her own person. When she was doing her school interview on Zoom she had me lying on the carpet trying to feed her answers. They asked her what she wanted for the future. I mouthed: *World peace, Sophia, world peace!* She ignored me and replied, 'A white Range Rover.' You go, girl.

Liberty is an angel with a wild streak. She's fun, quick, witty, always dancing around and singing. She loves her little brothers and is forever mothering them, dressing them up, applying make-up, pushing them around in prams. The way she plays is full of imagination.

Johnny's very mollycoddled because I supposed he'd be my last baby. When he was born I spent two weeks in bed with him, crying my eyes out and playing John Lennon's 'Beautiful Boy' on repeat. I couldn't believe how precious he was, and even now I treat him like a fragile piece of glass. He responds in kind and will spend hours just cuddling me and stroking my hair. He carries his king-size pillow everywhere and wants to be a dolphin-stroking mermaid when he grows up.

Peter: Who doesn't?

Abbey: And then there's Jack, who came out like a baby T-Rex. He's a boy's boy. He won't even countenance using a pink cup – *That's for girls!* – but he'll go nowhere without his skanky blanket, the most priceless possession we own. I don't even want to think about what would happen if we ever lost it.

Peter: When we had kids, we made a decision that we wouldn't change our lives too much. They would fit in with us. I definitely think they're better off for it. The kids could sleep on a building site because we never did the whole pitch-black and silent thing. They're friendly and adaptable and can get on with anybody, adults and children alike. And we're better off for it too.

Abbey: I never read any of the baby books. I took the view that ignorance is bliss. I think there's too much pressure on young mums to do everything a certain way. If you're not breastfeeding or playing them Mozart in the womb or putting them into a strict routine, you're somehow doing it wrong. I think that's nonsense. Every child is different, every parent is different, and it's important to make a plan that works for you rather than freaking yourself out for not going by the rules.

There's no doubt, though, that Pete and I have different parenting styles. No doubt that he loves to be good cop, leaving me to be bad cop. I want the teeth cleaned, the bedrooms tidied, the homework done. I want them to try harder. During lockdown, I'd be trying to get them to do their science assignments, and Pete would burst in and say, 'No one needs science! Who wants to go in the pool?'

You can predict the response: 'Yeah, Dad's the best!'

And when I lay down the law – 'No sweets until your homework's done!' – you can bet your bottom dollar that Pete will walk in like Willy Wonka and start handing out chocolate bars. 'Yeah, Dad's the best!'

In short, Pete does all the playing and I get all the shit jobs!

Peter: What can I say? Balance is important. Anybody want a Snickers?

L

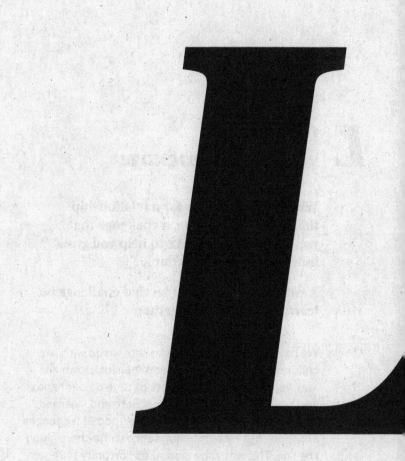

L is for earning a Language

What could be better for a relationship than a joint enterprise, a challenge that you can both undertake to help you grow individually and as a couple?

A word of advice: don't let that challenge be learning a language together.

Abbey: We have a house in Portugal where we go with the children every chance we get. When lockdown hit and we, like everyone, had lots of time on our hands, we thought it would be lovely if Pete and I learned Portuguese together. I used to be good at languages at school, but I lost my confidence somewhere along the line. This would be a good opportunity to regain it, and for Pete and me to do something fun as a couple.

It did not go to plan.

We found a tutor who would teach us online, and we managed to complete the grand total of one solitary, disastrous lesson.

The main trouble was that Pete held me back. There's a good chance I'd be fluent if it wasn't for him. He was so *slow* and unable to pronounce any of the words.

Peter: Actually, the main trouble was that Abbey kept finishing my sentences for me. I couldn't get a word in edgeways, so for most of the lesson I kept quiet. When I did try to talk, she'd stomp around the room complaining that I was taking too long and that I was too boring! So, actually, even though Abbey thinks she needed to be learning alongside someone more on her level, it's me who would be fluent if she'd only let me talk to the bloody teacher.

Abbey: We had a massive barney in front of the teacher. Pete told me to fuck off. I told Pete to fuck off. We never swear at each other, and here we were, playing fuck-off tennis. What a disaster!

The poor teacher claimed that we were both very good, very talented. Then she diplomatically suggested that, given our individual learning styles, we might benefit from separate lessons. Clearly she was desperate to put a stop to the domestic unfolding before her eyes.

To make matters worse, I'd prepared us a big pile of sausage sandwiches to keep us going through our marathon two-hour lesson. Unbeknown to us, our dog Jeffrey had scoffed the lot. So, in the space of less than an hour, we'd gone from being enthusiastic students to being on the verge of divorce and, even worse, starving!

Peter: *Obrigado*, Jeffrey.

L is for Love

Love comes in different packages. The most unlikely relationships are often the strongest. Does a relationship filled with banter and sarcasm, with jokes and jibes, mean less than a relationship that isn't?

Peter: Abbey and I spend a lot of time taking the mickey out of each other. We even do it in public. We even do it in this book! It's our thing, our schtick, a huge part of our relationship. But here's what counts: we could never be as free to take the piss out of each other if there wasn't a rock-solid foundation beneath it all. A relationship takes more than just laughter. It takes mutual respect. It takes shared morals. It takes a team-based approach to parenting. It takes attraction and friendship. In short, it takes love.

Abbey: When Pete and I first met, I think we both needed each other. We were both missing something in our lives, and it turns out that what I was missing was Pete, and what Pete was missing was me. It started off with the initial attraction, of course ...

Peter: There's no mystery why Abbey would be attracted to me, and happily I managed to see past her obvious physical disadvantages to find the beauty within ...

Abbey: But it quickly became clear that there was more to our relationship than that. We enjoyed each other's company so much from the off, and we acutely missed each other when we weren't together. Everyone has their ups and downs, of course, but 99 per cent of the time we never argued. We were best mates as well as boyfriend and girlfriend. And that's the most important thing about true love: it has friendship at its heart.

Peter: I think that to call your partner your best friend is the biggest compliment you can pay them. Abbey is definitely mine. I love my mates, and I love having a laugh with them. But Abbey's just as much fun as any of them, and she's my wife as well, so it's win-win. When we go away together, I have just as good a time as if I went away on a golf trip. And that's really saying something. Sadly, there are plenty of men who would not say that about their wives. I know guys, naming no names, who can't think of anything worse than going out for dinner with the missus. *I know she's just going to moan about school, talk about the bills ...*

Abbey: Whereas Pete and I don't really need anyone else. We like doing the same things and share the same sense of humour, and we complement each other well. I'm like a pitbull. If anyone ever says something bad about him, I'll kill 'em. I remember when he scored a goal and everyone said it was a fluke. I was on the warpath. *Fuck off, it wasn't a fluke. He's a professional footballer! Do you think he tried to score a goal by accident? Don't be ridiculous!* Say something like that about Pete and I'll fight you to the death.

Peter: It's quite nice having someone on your side like that, even if she does sometimes take it to extremes. I'm not always very good at sticking up for myself, so she'll take my phone and write assertive messages as if they're from me, but peppered with a smattering of distinctive Scouse. *Alright, mate, how's it going? YOU'VE GOT ONE MORE FUCKING CHANCE AT DOING THE FUCKING GARDEN. YOU'RE SHIT AT GARDENING. THE GARDEN'S DEAD. DO YOUR JOB OR YOU'RE FUCKING SACKED. Cheers, geezer, see you later!*

Abbey: And I know Pete's got my back, a hundred per cent, although he tends to be more of a calming influence. When I'm ready to go full-on pitbull, he's the voice of reason. The good angel on my shoulder while I'm the bad angel on his ...

Peter: Because sometimes I need a bad angel, and she needs a good one.

Abbey: The bottom line is, we adore each other, we protect each other and we always want to be together. The banter couldn't exist without the love. If Pete wasn't on this world, I wouldn't want to be on it either.

Peter: So in our book, that's what love's all about: being best friends who love each other's company and have each other's back. When you can do that, you can take the piss as much as you like ...

M

M is for Make-up Sex

There has to be something that makes an argument worthwhile, right? But how do you have make-up sex if you're not very good at making up?

Peter: Make-up sex. I have heard tell of this mythical activity. I've read about it in books. I've seen it in films. And I like the idea of having a fiery argument and hurling stuff at each other, before passionately ripping off each other's clothes and making the earth move. But I can categorically say that it has never happened in this house.

Abbey: Make-up sex doesn't exist for stubborn people, because first you have to make up, and we're not very good at doing that. It's a Mexican stand-off in the Crouch-Clancy household after an argument. Pete's not one of life's natural apologisers. He's not the sort of man who suddenly says, 'Darling, I'm sorry. I was wrong and you were right. You are *always* right.' In 17 years, I don't think he's said sorry once.

He goes about it in a different way, by performing little acts of kindness that I have to keep an eye out for. The other night I got a 'bin apology'. We'd been making digs at each other all night, and when the digs stopped I didn't get a 'sorry' but I did notice that Pete took the rubbish out *and* replaced the bin bags. That act was as good a sorry as I could have hoped for.

I'm also familiar with the 'cup of tea apology'. This involves the tactful delivery of unasked-for tea and biscuits before bed. It is an unspoken truce, one of those small gestures and tiny acts of selflessness that he deploys to worm his way back into my good books.

However, Pete is not always prepared to make one of these meaningful gestures. If he's not ready to forgive and forget when bedtime comes around, he brings out the big guns: the punishment pyjamas. Normally he goes to bed naked (easy, ladies), but if he thinks that I need a punishment, he wears full pyjamas. The silence is heavy as he purposefully buttons up his PJs in protest. *Sorry, babe – you've done it this time. You don't get to see my beautiful bare arse tonight!*

I love the idea that his gorgeous body and lovely buttocks are only a reward if I've been good.

Peter: It's news to me that I've ever deployed my pyjamas as a punishment. But I might do it more regularly now. What a way of letting Abbey know that I'm fuming. 'You won't get so much as a glimpse of this magnificent work of art tonight ...' It's no wonder make-up sex hasn't featured much in our house.

M is for May as Well Move in Together

It starts with having a spare toothbrush and emergency knickers at your boyfriend's house for when you stay the night, and before you know it you're never not there. Move in together? May as well, I suppose.

Abbey: When I first walked into Pete's flat, I couldn't believe my eyes. It was like something from *The Inbetweeners*. He was 24 years old at the time and playing for Liverpool, but he still kept his loose change in a *Loaded* magazine money box covered in naked girls on his bedside table. He had a single fold-up camping bed in one room and used the other as a sort of 'dressing room'. There was no wardrobe, just one of those little metal racks with all his clothes hung up on show. His T-shirts, pants and socks were all piled in the corner.

Who on earth is this bloke, I thought, *and why is he living like a teenager*?

There was no real linen on the bed, just a faded mismatch of baby-blue flower-printed sheets that I presumed his mum must have given him.

No wonder he's single! I thought.

Peter: In my defence, I was only ever there for a few hours a day. I would get up and head out every morning for training and close the door on it. I didn't really care about decorating or even getting the most basic items of furniture. It was just a place to sleep, and I couldn't see the point of doing anything to it. The bed was long enough that my feet didn't poke out the end, and that was enough for me.

I chose the place because it was close to my gran. She lived around the corner and looked after me. Sometimes she would pop round and cook me dinner, or she'd clean my clothes when the piles of washing on the floor grew taller than me. I didn't really need much. I could have gone all flash and brought a personal chef in, if I'd really thought about it, or if I'd been bothered. I could have employed cleaners to scrub the bath. But Gran was just round the corner, so I'd cram my laundry into a bin bag and take it round to hers to have it all washed for me. Lifesaver, really, because I didn't know how to use a dishwasher. I'd never had to wash sheets.

Abbey: A dishwasher? For your sheets? That's the level of domestic competence I was dealing with. Still am!

Peter kept a bag of dry pasta in the fridge rather than in a cupboard, along with a jar of pesto and some chorizo. We had Pete's special chorizo pesto pasta most nights. If we were feeling particularly sophisticated we'd add a few black olives. Pete often seemed to pick up a jar of those. Or maybe it was the same jar that had been festering there for months. Honestly I don't want to think about it. Either way, black olives were the pièce de résistance for fusilli à la Crouchi.

There was an old sofa in the sitting room and frankly not much else. The only thing that wasn't on its last legs was the absolutely massive TV that wouldn't have looked out of place in the local Odeon. He wasn't a footballer for nothing!

All in all, it wasn't exactly a palace. But it was full of happy memories for us, and when he asked me to move in, it became my home too.

As a girl, being asked to move in with your boyfriend is a big deal. A real sign of the commitment you are making to one another. An acknowledgement that you love each other so much that you can't bear to spend a single day apart. I had imagined that when the time came there would be a grand gesture. Maybe Pete would take me out for dinner and give me a box with his front-door key in it. I'd even daydreamed that it might be engraved with a romantic, meaningful message: *You've got the key to my heart, so here's the key to my flat*. It would be a moment for us to look back on years later and maybe even tell the children about.

But no. There was no deep and meaningful conversation where we made plans for our future. There was no engraving. There was a text. It said: 'You may as well move in.'

I wish I still had that text: a memento of possibly the least romantic moment of my life. It certainly didn't scream 'I can't live without you!'

Peter: As a bloke, I had no clue that a romantic gesture was required, or even that it would be welcome. No one teaches you that moving in is 'a thing'. I pondered the question for literally a second before texting her. I apologised afterwards, but at the time I just thought, *Well, she's here all the time anyway and it's been great, so why not?* Abbey had been living at her mum's, where the sitting room was always full of her little brothers and sisters, so we'd end up camping out in her bedroom like a couple of teenagers. It just made sense for her to move in.

Abbey: Moving in with Pete felt so fun, and totally different from how I'd imagined. It was such a novelty, like we were playing house. I was 19 years old at the time, but I loved cleaning the house, putting on a little pinny and flapping out the tea towels. While Pete was at work I made that place immaculate. I bought a new bed, some sheets that actually matched and even some real pillows. The house was transformed.

Peter: I remember coming in from training and opening the door to find the lights on and the whole place looking and feeling so much brighter. It even smelt different. Suddenly there were flowers, and there was actual food. It wasn't just chorizo pesto pasta, or one of the many thousands of frozen meals I'd bought for myself over the years. She would make green juices in a blender with cucumber, spinach and kale. She used actual vegetables in recipes – not just peas on the side for garnish. While I barely knew how to turn the hob on, she'd be chopping and boiling and grilling things.

Abbey: I used to like to get all dressed up for when Pete came home. He'd walk in and I'd be making dinner in a pair of high heels. Things have changed now – he's lucky if I even have a moment to give him a proper hello, and the only food I'll have prepared is the couple of slices of cold pizza left over from the kids' supper.

Peter: I'd get back from training in the early afternoon, home by two o'clock, and we'd have some sort of delicious lunch that Abbey had prepared, followed by a lovely nap together. An afternoon nap is one of life's biggest luxuries these days. We used to make up a bed on the floor next to the fire, draw the curtains and watch box sets and back-to-back films. It was as near to heaven as you could get.

Abbey: We had fallen so in love. We didn't have much of the day apart, but we'd miss each other when we weren't together.

Peter: All in all, despite my underwhelming invitation, moving in together was such a seamless transition. I might have had my faults, but there was not one single thing about Abbey that annoyed me. No bad habit that you find out about your partner after they move in. No weird quirks that I had to learn to live with. I loved the whole package and I still do, all these years later.

M is for My Side of the Bed

The bedtime routine. It should be calming, peaceful. It should set you up for a restful night's sleep so that you can awake refreshed and ready to tackle another day.

But some bedtime routines are not quite like that ...

Peter: First things first. It's an unwritten rule that each partner in the relationship has their own side of the bed, right? To sleep on the wrong side would be unthinkable. You just couldn't do it. And it's an organic thing, the decision as to who sleeps on which side. It happens naturally ...

Abbey: Wrong. I chose my side of the bed because it was the furthest from the door, so if a burglar broke in he'd have to get past you first.

Peter: Unfortunately, Abbey's reckless attitude towards this fundamental law of nature has upset an already precarious night-time routine. She'll go up a bit before me while I lock up (I like to think of myself as the security guy) and deal with the dog. I make Abbey her cup of tea and biscuit, bring it up to the bedroom, and what do I find? Abbey, phone in hand as she deals with her emails, on *my side of the bed*. An absolutely catastrophic upending of the natural order.

Abbey: There's method in my madness. I like to have my phone in my left hand and my cup of tea and biscuit within reach of my right hand. That means having the bedside table to my right. And that means lying on Pete's side of the bed.

Peter: So I think to myself, *That's OK. It's no big deal. She can stay there until I've brushed my teeth and applied my Elemis Pro-Collagen Marine Cream (because I'm worth it).* So I make my ablutions, wander back in – and she's still there. Clearly I can't get in on her side, but it seems a bit petty, asking her to move. So I plug in my phone, fold my clothes, deal with the floordrobe, but pretty soon I've run out of jobs. I hover a bit. I pace up and down the room ...

Abbey: He'll walk in, he'll walk out. Sometimes he'll go and do a hundred sit-ups, to the point where I wonder who he's trying to impress and accuse him of having an affair. He could just get into my side of the bed for a bit, but that doesn't seem to be an option.

Peter: Of *course* it's not an option. My polite requests that she migrate to her side of the bed go unheeded. So recently, I've hit on a more diplomatic strategy to resolve the situation. I place Abbey's tea and biscuit on *her* bedside table. The lure of the biscuit is too strong for her. She'll do anything for a Rich Tea. As she succumbs to the irresistible pull of the night-time snack, I jump into my side and all is well with the world.

Except all isn't quite well with the world, because actually my side of the bed is the absolute worst. It's got a big dip in it, and a sharp spring poking out like a dagger. It's like being attacked by a sabre-toothed tiger in the middle of the night. I sometimes wake up in the morning with gashes all over my skin. Each time it happens, I can't help thinking to myself, *We've done well enough not to be living like this ...*

Abbey: But we only ever think of it when we're in bed. Once we're up and about, we forget all about the lethal spring. It's not until we get back into bed again that we remember we need a new fucking mattress ...

Peter: And that I'm going to be stabbed in the leg all night.

Abbey: So now, eventually, we're in bed, each on the correct side, Pete wincing in pain. We'll easily spend an hour looking through Netflix, deciding what we want to watch ...

Peter: Nightmare.

Abbey: Then at least one of the kids will come in, probably two, maybe three.

Peter: It's like Piccadilly Circus.

Abbey: And to top it all, we'll normally have the cat on the duvet, chucking up a hairball.

So that's our bedtime routine. Calming, peaceful and restful it is not.

Agony ~~Aunt~~ Ab

Dear Abbey,

I hope you can help me with something that has been bugging me for a while ... I have absolutely no idea how to approach the situation.

It concerns my boyfriend's table manners – he simply does not have any! Every time we share a meal, regardless of where, be it Maccie D's or a Michelin-star restaurant, he leaves me majorly cringing.

Not only does he, quite literally, fail to grasp how to correctly hold a knife and fork, but he also seems to think it's completely acceptable to chew and talk with his mouth wide open. It's got to the point that whenever he suggests going out for a romantic meal I shudder at the thought of having to stare into his food-filled gob while he tells me how great I look that night.

It doesn't stop there. Once we finish, he proceeds to suck and pick at any stray food left in his teeth. It's like an 80-year-old grandad sucking on a Werther's Original.

I do love my boyfriend, and, in the grand scheme of things, I know this is only minor, but it is seriously starting to give me the ick!

How can I tell him that his eating habits resemble those of a five-year-old without hurting his feelings and risking never being taken on a date night again?

Ellie, 25 – Brighton

Abbey: Manners are everything to me. Our kids are always getting up and walking around in the middle of meals, so it's a battle in my house, but I think having good manners is so important. The last thing I want is for my children to grow up with bad table manners.

Peter: They are an important thing for our family with the kids, but they're even more important when you are an adult. How would you feel if I was incredible in absolutely every other way, but I spoke with my mouth full and shovelled my food down me?

Abbey: I have to admit that I shovel my food down a bit. I am a fast eater. I also hold my knife and fork in the wrong hands. In my defence, when I was younger I was never told which hands to hold the knife and fork in correctly, and now it has kind of stuck. My dad even licks the plate, so I think I've done remarkably well!

Ellie, perhaps a subtle way to help improve your boyfriend's table manners is to watch *Pretty Woman* together. Your boyfriend could learn a lot from the scene where Vivian is taught which cutlery to use. But I also don't think there's anything wrong with taking a more blunt approach, and saying, 'You eat like a pig. Sort it out.' After all, when it comes to relationships, there are so many special occasions when you would ordinarily go for a meal: Valentine's Day, birthdays, anniversaries, date nights. If you are trying to get in a romantic mood and your partner is eating like a pig across the table, it's not going to end well, so you have to address it.

Peter: Anything romantic involves a meal, so let's be honest, if you have bad table manners you're never going to get lucky and be on the receiving end of a beaver emoji, are you?

N

N is for the Name Game

It's easy to make a wish-list of baby names as long as your arm. But what happens when you actually meet the baby? And how do you make sure you don't saddle them with a nickname they'll never shake?

Abbey: We used to lie in bed for hours on end playing the name game. We played it long before we had any babies to name, or any animals, for that matter. We'd take it in turns to suggest a name and see how it landed with the other person. Often we'd both recoil in horror as we remembered people who had crossed our paths with the same name. Because, let's face it, you don't want to name your daughter after the playground bully, or your son after your mate's embarrassing dad. And what works for a baby when they're all cute and tiny doesn't necessarily work for the barrister or doctor you hope they might become.

Even so, well before we had kids we had a list so long we'd have been able to name the entire farm's worth of animals I was convinced I'd one day have.

We chose slightly more unusual names for the girls than for the boys. I've always loved posh, princess-y names like Saskia and, of course, Sophia. My favourite girl's name has always been Allegra, but unfortunately when you marry a six-foot-seven giant, Allegra is off the menu.

Peter: Can you imagine it? 'Over here, Leggy! How are you doing, Leggy? Have you met Leggy? She's five-foot-eleven with legs up to her armpits.' I've always been teased about my height and grew up being called 'lanky' or 'beanpole'. Then, of course, there's the small matter of 40,000 fans singing, 'He's big, he's red, his feet stick out the bed ... Peter Crouch!' at the top of their voices. As it's a fair bet that any daughter of mine and Abs will be tall, I didn't want to supply either of them with a ready-made nickname like Leggy. So, in the end, we chose Sophia and Liberty, which we love.

Abbey: Boys' names come with their own set of challenges. I think both parents look for something different. The mum might want a romantic hero who's going to sweep the girls off their feet, whereas the dad might want a solid, dependable name that suggests a good bloke you'd want to go to the pub with.

Peter: In the end we went for Johnny and Jack. Nothing controversial there, surely? No own goals for them to blame us for.

Abbey: Despite the long list we compiled playing the name game, Jack didn't even have a name for about a month. We originally thought he'd be Teddy, short for Edward, but it just wasn't him. He was sweet and gorgeous, but somehow not a Teddy. We toyed around with Kit, but decided that Kit Crouch sounds like a football kit. And Freddy Crouch just made us think of Freddy Krueger. It turns out Crouch is a tricky surname to deal with. Eventually, time was running out because we had to register the birth. Our friends were waiting with bated breath. With all the build-up they imagined we were plotting something original and unusual. Bentley? Drake? Maverick? I think they were a bit disappointed that they'd waited all that time for 'Jack'.

What can I say? The name game is much easier to play before you've actually met your kids ...

N is for Not Talking Shop

Break out the world's smallest violin, because it's a tough old gig being a footballer, especially when the world and his wife want to talk shop. Thankfully, Pete and Abbey have that sorted ...

Peter: There were periods during my career when I played well. There were periods when I didn't play well. And there were periods when I was in good form but just couldn't get the minutes on the pitch. For a while at Liverpool, I was in the best sporting condition of my life, but I kept getting benched. It was upsetting, but I always tried not to bring a negative attitude home with me.

Abbey was always brilliant at helping me with that. She'd talk about something different the moment I walked through the door. It wasn't because she has no interest in football (although by now you know her thoughts on the beautiful game). She just knew that the last thing I'd want to talk about was how the match had gone and why I'd spent most of it sitting on that bloody bench.

There are players who love nothing more than mulling over every nuance of the game. They dissect every angle, every ball, every shot, every missed opportunity, every tackle. And they do it for *every game*. I don't see the point in worrying about something you can't change when you get home. Trust me: the club would go over it endlessly with the players in any case. You can't bury a bad performance, but until you're back on the training pitch, what's done is done. I'd rather be talking about the children's homework than going over every kick of the ball from a game that's in the past.

Abbey: I wanted to respect that, but it was an unusual stance to take. It's amazing how involved some of the partners are. Whenever I went to the players' lounge (which wasn't often), I couldn't get my head around how some of the wives acted. As soon as the players had cooled down and had a shower, the wives would have a go at them for a weak tackle or a loose pass. I'd just smile and say, 'Babe, where should we go for dinner tonight?'

Peter: Abbey's ability to not talk shop was a godsend. Even now, everywhere I go, somebody wants to talk shop with me. I'll pop out for a pint of milk and a guy will stop to talk football. I'll fill the car up and the attendant will want to know who's the greatest player of all time. I'll go to buy some sausages and the butcher will want to know why Grealish is on the bench. It's nice to come home to a football-free zone!

Abbey: Occasionally, I wouldn't mind talking about the day I've had at work, but Pete has as much interest in my modelling as I do in the offside rule. To him, all I do is get my hair, nails and make-up done and then tit around with the glam squad in front of a camera.

Peter: Make-up and a few snaps, that's basically it, isn't it? You mess around taking pictures and I mess around with my mates kicking a ball around a field. Let's try not to bring it home with us, hey?

O

O is for Old

For better or worse. For richer or poorer. In sickness and in health. What does it all mean? Does it mean loving one another when we've become cantankerous old farts sitting in rocking chairs? Or is it possible to look forward to the inevitable business of growing old?

Abbey: Pete and I can't wait to grow old together. Count us in! Although, we're not quite on the same page about where and how to spend those golden-oldie years. I'd like to live on a farm somewhere deeply rural. Pete wants to play golf until they wheel him off the ninth hole in a box. But that's OK. He could go and play golf all day and I could hang out with the animals. Everyone's a winner! I could even embrace my inner Brigitte Bardot and open an animal sanctuary. Imagine it – all those horses, donkeys, goats ...

Peter: Rural farm, fine. Me playing golf all day, fine. But I draw the line at goats.

Abbey: If it's not goats, it'll have to be donkeys. I'll open a sanctuary for all the old donkeys who have retired from taking kids on rides along the sea front. That's the dream. An old age with old donkeys. Who could ask for more?

Most of all, though, I'm looking forward to being a grandparent – a really hands-on grandparent, up to my elbows in toddlers and helping out as much as I can. Some couples make plans to downsize when their kids are all grown up, but I want us to have a place that's big enough for all our kids and their own families to come and stay. Imagine it: all the children running around playing games. It will be our very own version of *The Waltons*.

Peter: It's why people get married, isn't it? So they can start a family and grow old together. So they can take on life's highs and lows as a team. I'm not totally certain that everyone sees donkey sanctuaries in their future plans, but I guess I could learn to live with that as long as we were tackling life together.

Sometimes I wonder what we'll look like. I can really picture Abbey decked out with her half-moon granny spectacles and her hand-knitted cardigan, comfy slippers and a rug over her knees.

Abbey: Ain't gonna happen. I want to be a hot, glamorous granny.

Peter: A hot, glamorous granny with donkeys? I'm in.

P

P is for *acking and Planning*

There's packing, there's planning ...

And then there's Pete.

Abbey: If we're going away as a family, I start packing *months* in advance. The whole landing will be covered with open suitcases and I'll do a little bit each day. Every suitcase has to be super-organised. Everything must be colour-coordinated, so the blue shirts are all together, then the white shirts, then Pete's towelling Gucci combos. There are spares for each day, there are military-grade medical packs with antibiotics, inhalers and painkillers. There are baby bags, iPads, chargers ... Not only that, but each suitcase must hold enough variety of outfits for all six of us in case the rest of the luggage goes missing, a bit like the president and vice president never travelling on the same plane. Everything has to be perfect. The idea of it *not* being perfect gives me full-on anxiety.

Peter: When we arrive at the airport as a family, it looks like we're moving house. In all fairness, Abbey's packing is a truly wondrous thing. A masterpiece of planning and precision. It always amazes me how she manages to get all six of us sorted. But it comes at a cost: this kind of high-level organisation takes time, so the planning for the return journey starts on about day two of the holiday. Our holiday conversation revolves around the packing. We'll talk about it incessantly as the clock ticks away. *I've got to pack in five days. Just four more days till I start packing ...*

Abbey: It's a burden. I sometimes find myself thinking, *I bet Elton John doesn't pack his own bag.* I want a packer, like Elton!

Peter: But it would never work. Abbey would never be able to leave them alone. She'd have to monitor them constantly.

Abbey: Maybe I'm a control freak.

Peter: Do you think? Has that only just occurred to you?

Abbey: Well, if I am, it's not mean control-freakery. But it does irk me slightly that Peter and I have such wildly different approaches to packing.

Peter: If I go away on a golf trip, I'll start thinking about what to pack approximately half an hour before leaving for the airport. Which I think gives me plenty of time. When Abbey was last pregnant, I took the kids on holiday by myself. Abbey wanted us to come back with our clean clothes and dirty clothes split between different cases. Suffice to say that, while we were away, Abbey's packing regime went to the wall. We did not start planning it on day two. We'd come back from the beach and chuck our dirty stuff into a big pile. The kids felt so liberated! Free as a bird! We sent daily pictures of the ever-increasing dirty clothes pile to Abbey back home ...

Abbey: And I thought I'd go into early labour with the stress of it. Unfortunately, our son Jack hasn't inherited his mum's packing style. When we let him pack his own bag for holiday, he filled it with pen knives and bottle openers and rocks from the garden. That was an interesting trip through security. I try very hard to make everything perfect, but somehow it all seems to descend into chaos ...

Peter: I have to take my share of the blame. Once, when we had a new baby, we decided to go to a country show for the day. Abbey packed everything we needed: baby bag, milk bottle, pram, nappies. We got to the show, and two hours in, the baby needed feeding and changing. No problem. Abbey's got it sorted.

Except ... the baby bag, milk bottle, pram and nappies were still sitting by the front door at home. I had one job – to put the gear in the car – and I'd fallen short. My oversight went down as well as could be expected, especially when we had to drive into the nearest town centre to buy milk, nappies and a new pram. I did feel a bit bad about that one.

Abbey: Don't believe a word of it.

My obsession with proper packing extends to unloading the groceries into the fridge. Everything has to be in its proper place. The yoghurt on the yoghurt shelf. The meat on the meat shelf. The fruit on the fruit shelf. When I ask Pete to unload the shopping, he just chucks it in and the fridge looks like a bomb's hit it. Now he's not allowed anywhere near the shopping. I'm not fooled by his strategic incompetence. I know he's just doing a job badly so he won't be asked to do it again. But my need for perfect packing won't let me take the fight to him.

Peter: No comment.

P is for Parties

Stick the beers in the ice bath and put the music on loud.

And in the Clancy–Crouch house, that's just for the kids' parties ...

Abbey: I love hosting parties. I'd far rather have people over for drinks at home than go out anywhere. It just makes me happy seeing everyone having a good time. And it's children's parties that really float my boat.

When I was young – if we were really lucky – we'd go for a Wimpy burger.

Peter: I still don't think you can beat a Wimpy party with burgers, chips and a pint of Coke. I always thought they were absolute perfection. You can keep your bouncy castles and your children's entertainers.

Abbey: Now I set my sights a little higher. I go all-out. Full-on Kardashian, with fancy cakes and over-the-top decorations. I want the children to remember their parties and talk about them long after they're all grown up. And I'm making up for the time we lost during the pandemic, when none of us could have a party unless we lived in Downing Street. I want to bring some magic back into the kids' lives. For Liberty, I held a Pamper Party Festival, with tents for hair-braiding and manicures. The kids went wild for all the potions and lotions as they swanned about in fluffy bathrobes, all pampered and living their best lives. We had the most amazing cakes and even a mocktail masterclass. Admittedly they did all end up spending most of the time in the pool, so I could have had the party for free. But don't try to tell me a Wimpy lunch is better than that.

Peter: Cheeseburgers? Ketchup sachets? It's a close call ...

Of course, when you throw a kids' party, you aren't just looking after the twenty-odd children. You're looking after their parents too. And once the children's entertainer has done their bit and the parents have been enjoying a mid-afternoon glass of wine, it's at the after-party that things can really get raucous. Last year, one mum jumped into the pool. And, of course, once one person enters the pool, the seal is broken and that's it: everyone's jumping in. What was a relatively civilised children's event starts to resemble an Ibiza pool party.

On another occasion we started a game of volleyball that became so competitive it went on for nearly nine hours. The sun set over the garden and we had to drive the cars onto the lawn so we could use their headlamps as makeshift floodlights. Nothing was going to stop us from seeing that volleyball tournament through, even if it did mean we were still playing past midnight. All the kids were there, and Abbey's mum was one of the last ones standing, which I suppose explains where she gets her love of a party from.

Abbey: Good vibes.

P is for Posh Kids

They say the apple doesn't fall far from the tree, and in many ways our kids are just like us. But when it comes to the lifestyle they lead compared to the one their parents were used to, they might just have landed in a whole other orchard.

And that's OK ...

Abbey: I remember hearing Ronaldo talk about his children in an interview. He was responding to the suggestion that he spoiled his kids. His response was along the following lines: 'I grew up playing football on streets covered in rubbish. I worked hard to get where I am, and now that I have all this privilege, how could I not put my kids into the best schools I can find, and give them the best opportunities life has to offer? I want them to have all the things I didn't. How stupid would I be not to do the best for them?'

I never saw myself taking life advice from a footballer – apart from the one I live with, of course – but I thought he spoke a lot of sense.

Everything moves on. My dad only used to get a bath once a week, which he took in the back garden. He was one of three kids and he was always last into the tub, by which time it was black and freezing. Can you imagine how cold it must have been in winter? My nan would spit on a tissue that she used to wipe down his face, so he would stink of spit. She called it a 'pussycat wash'. My upbringing was a million miles from that, and our children's upbringing has evolved even further.

It's a normal process. I once took part in the cooking reality-TV show *Hell's Kitchen*, and Barry McGuigan, the boxer, was a fellow contestant. He's proper Irish and yet when his children came to visit him during filming they had such posh English accents. It was the first time I'd come across anyone having such a different accent to their parent's so it was quite a shock.

As a toddler, Sophia had a thick Scouse accent. You'd think she'd been born within sight of the liver birds. She's completely different now. She has a cut-glass accent with no hint of Scouse. So, when it comes to talking, my kids are definitely a lot posher than I am. And that's OK, because things move on. I want to give our kids everything: a lovely house, the best education, all the opportunities that I didn't have myself when I was growing up.

But if I'm fortunate enough to be able to give them these things, that's what I want to do. In fact, I think it's *especially* understandable that you might want to give them all these advantages if you grew up without them.

I still want them to have ambition, though. To work for things, like we had to. That's why I was so keen for Sophia to swim when we found out she had a real talent for it. I wanted her to see that not everything is easy and you can't just pay for the life you want. You have to work for success and happiness too. Swimming training was good for developing the discipline of working hard and getting rewarded for it. She'd come back exhausted from training after swimming for hours, and I'd tell her, 'That's life. You've got to dedicate your time to something and keep going at it even when things get tough. When you've got a job to do, you have to stick with it. You can't just wake up one morning and say, "I don't feel like going in today."'

I'm always trying to teach our kids that work ethic: that nothing worthwhile is ever easy, and it's an unbeatable feeling when you try hard and – with some perseverance – succeed.

And I don't want them to grow up living a life that is so far removed from where we came from that it's impossible for them to connect on some level. My dad was horrified when he found out that they were going to have Westminster listed on their birth certificates. He kept asking why we couldn't just come home to Liverpool for the birth, so they'd always have proof of their Liverpool heritage.

Peter: I think it's cool to be born in Westminster! It's where the Royal Family live, W1, the centre of London. They can still say they're half Liverpudlian, and they still have family there. I think there's a happy medium, and your children will always be a reflection of your own experiences and values. We spend so much time together as a family that our children have naturally turned out to be very similar to us in how they talk and what they care about. Even though we live in Surrey, we try to keep Liverpool alive for them as part of their background. They're Scousers at heart, and I care about them supporting the football club their dad played for!

Abbey: The house we live in is their reality. It's very privileged, but it's still important to manage expectations. I'm conscious of the need to say no to things rather than always saying yes. It's so important that the kids learn that they can't get what they want *all* the time. Pete, on the other hand, is a 'yes man'. If they walk past a shop and ask for something, Pete always says yes.

Peter: I'm incredibly proud of them all. That's why it's so hard not to say yes to everything they ask for!

Abbey: At the end of the day, though, they are the best kids. Not spoiled brats, by any means. They have a bit of attitude, but some attitude is good. It makes you feisty and strong. It means you won't let anyone push you around.

P is for Proposing

Is there anything more romantic than a proposal? Down on bended knee, ring in hand and the weight of expectation hanging in the air. Will she say yes?

So how did Abbey and Pete's proposal pan out? It wasn't simple, that's for sure ...

Abbey: Pete is absolutely adamant that I drew the engagement ring I wanted on the back of a napkin, so that he would be absolutely certain about what I liked. I don't remember doing that at all, but I will say this: if I *did* draw it, it wasn't to scale. Pete's got no time for jewellery (see D is for Diamonds), so I suppose I shouldn't have expected a massive piece of bling. There is a diamond there, but you need to get your glasses out to see it ...

Peter: Abbey definitely *did* draw a ring on the back of a napkin. Very wise too. The last thing either of us would want is for me to go rogue when it comes to engagement-ring shopping. I would definitely have buggered it up without a blueprint, but a scrawl on the back of a pub napkin was only ever going to get me so far. I've always preferred spending money on experiences rather than things, especially jewellery, so I didn't really know where to start.

Abbey: Would it help if I said that the *experience* of putting on a big, beautiful ring every day is pretty exciting for me?

Peter: As for the proposal itself, I had it all planned. The season was over and I had a month off, so I organised this amazing trip. Abbey and I would travel the world during the summer break. There would be a whirlwind trip to the Big Apple. We would take in some of the most beautiful European islands. And to round off this holiday of a lifetime, the cherry on the cake, I would ask her to marry me. I would get down on one knee, bring out the bling, and pop the question. What could be more romantic?

Abbey: I knew something was up when I reached for his bag as we were waiting to take off for New York. He dived across a whole row of passengers to grab it back off me. Clearly the bag contained something he didn't want me to see, and I was certain it was a ring.

I knew the proposal was coming ...

Throughout the holiday, we'd go out for fabulous dinners every night at restaurants Pete had booked in advance. Every night I thought, *This is it!* I'd be done up to death, with photoshoot-level hair, make-up and heels. The full works. I'd sit there at dinner with a huge smile on my face, just waiting for the moment when he'd get down on one knee.

The moment didn't come.

Each night we'd finish dinner with no ring, no bended knee, no big question. My heart started to sink. My smile would fade. My shoulders would sag. Pete would say, 'Wasn't that meal incredible? Did you enjoy the food? How about that view?' And I'd be a moody old cow: 'I wouldn't bother going back there again. It was fine if you had no choice ...'

With each passing night, my mood grew worse. Poor Pete must have thought I was so ungrateful as he took me to unbelievably beautiful places, picturesque restaurants overlooking gorgeous marinas, with little boats and twinkling lights under the breathtaking night skies. We dined up mountains and in stunning private coves. At each of these incredible meals I'd be thinking, *This is the perfect place for a proposal.*

But still, the proposal never came.

We arrived in Ibiza, our final destination. We'd been on holiday for 25 days and he still hadn't asked me to marry him. Now we'd arranged for a group of friends to join us, so as far as I was concerned, the proposal was off. I was so upset that I'd got it so wrong – all I wanted to do was go home and have a good cry. When we arrived at our pretty villa, Pete had booked me a surprise massage. It was the last thing I wanted! I was tense and grumpy, and a massage wasn't going to solve anything. Little did I know that the massage was a ploy to get rid of me while Pete prepared another surprise ...

After the massage I was upstairs on our balcony, fuming and putting off getting dressed for the dreaded evening ahead. I was wondering if the future even held anything for us when I heard Pete calling me from downstairs: 'Are you dressed yet? Can you come down?'

I wasn't dressed and I didn't want to go down. But I decided to face the music and stomped down in my PJs with wet hair. I walked into the sitting room and I couldn't believe my eyes.

There were hundreds of candles dotted around the room. There were pink rose petals scattered everywhere. It was beautiful. And there was Pete, finally down on one knee, holding a little red box.

I burst into tears, overwhelmed by the romance of it all.

Peter: She cried so much that she couldn't answer when I asked her to marry me. She was so taken aback by what I'd done to the room that she called her mum and started filming it. 'Look at this room, Mum! Look at this ring!' I stood there like a lemon, thinking, *I presume that's a yes? She hasn't said no, anyway ...*

Abbey: Suddenly, I could see how thoughtfully he'd planned the whole thing. Our friends were arriving right after the proposal so we could have a big party in the villa together. He'd even told my family and friends back in Liverpool what he was planning, so they were all together having an engagement party of their own!

Peter: It's funny how life turns out. I wanted that ring to be on her finger for a good long time before we actually got married. I wanted to enjoy being engaged, to have some fun with it. But soon after the proposal we found out that, having spent years trying to conceive, Abbey was pregnant with Sophia.

Abbey: The pieces were all falling into place. No sooner had we gone from committing to spending our lives together than a third little member of our family was on the way.

Agony ~~Aunt~~ Ab

Dear Abbey,

I love your podcast, and after listening to the advice you've given people in similar situations, I decided to bite the bullet and write in myself.

My problem is how vain my husband has become. Throughout our 11-year marriage he has always taken care of himself – dressing smartly, smelling nice – but he has definitely remained on the 'man's man' end of the scale.

Last year, though, he decided to do something about his 'dad bod', and since then he has become almost insufferable. He has managed to lose a lot of weight, but his full-on skincare routine is starting to put mine to shame and he spends hours styling the three strands of hair he has left on his head. It's like he thinks he's a James Dean-style heartthrob when, in reality, he's probably more James Martin (and that's being generous).

I'm sorry, but I do not want my hubby spending more time getting ready for a night on the tiles than I do. He should be trying to get me out the door, not the other way around.

Help me get my man back!

Holly, 36 – Cardiff

Abbey: Vanity in a man is a major turn-off for me. I didn't turn up for a date once because the guy I was meeting had called me beforehand to tell me all about the outfit he had planned to wear, right down to the beaded bracelets to match his shirt.

I like a man to be a man. I think they should exercise and maintain their body and look after themselves, but I've never even seen Peter look in the mirror, and if he started checking his reflection out endlessly before we went out that would give me the ick.

Peter: I'm not sure a man can win in this situation. If you take care of yourself, you're vain, but if you don't take care of yourself, you've let yourself go. It's a fine line you have to tread.

Abbey: There is definitely a very fine line between taking care of yourself and then going and buying the whole collection from Gucci, though, Pete. The Gucci co-ord you bought is more suitable for a 20-something Premier League footballer, not a balding 42-year-old man. That screams midlife crisis to me.

Peter: That's harsh – you told me I look gorgeous in that outfit! What advice can we give to Holly?

Abbey: Holly, I think your husband needs a reality check. It's all good and well that he's got himself fit and lost the dad bod. You want him looking good, but it sounds like you need to bring him down a few pegs. Tell him that he's not a ten, he's just about a six.

Peter: So, you're basically advocating that Holly belittles her husband and ruins his confidence?

Abbey: Correct.

Q

Q is for BBQ Pete

The sun shines for the first day of summer and men all over the country dust off their trusty tongs, don their aprons, crack open a cold beer and a packet of sausages, and fire up the barbecue. Pete's no exception ...

Abbey: What is it about a barbecue that turns every man into a budding Jamie Oliver? As soon as the barbie comes out, Pete discovers a sudden passion for cooking. Not *real* cooking, of course. You won't find him in the kitchen chopping garlic and mixing spices to make a zingy marinade. He's not the type to baste a chicken leg or slather a special hot sauce over the sausages. He won't be slow-roasting the pork over the embers of a smouldering fire.

For Pete, the preparation is limited to a trip to the butcher and the removal of the packaging. Then he'll throw the sausages and burgers on the barbecue all at the same time, and hope for the best. If we're lucky, he might flip a skewer or two. If we're unlucky, he'll eat half the food he's barbecuing all by himself.

As a less-than-expert chef, Pete always gets the quantities wrong. I once asked him to go to the butchers to get something nice for the barbie for dinner. He came back with four wild boar sausages. *Four?!* Don't get me wrong, they looked lovely, but four was never going to be enough, especially as I was pregnant and starving. They must have seen him coming. When I turned my nose up at his efforts, he got annoyed and threw them out of the window. At least, he tried to. The window was shut, the sausages were raw and they slid slowly down the glass like something out of an old-fashioned Punch and Judy sketch.

Of course, not all men are barbecue klutzes. Our friend Robin is incredible: he'll roast a whole chicken on a rotisserie over smoky coals for hours. And I'm not much better than Pete. Our barbecue style is more along the lines of burnt, with a lovely raw middle to mix things up.

I wish we were better, to be honest. If I had my time out there in the dating world again, I think I'd put 'good at barbecuing' on my marriage checklist.

Peter: I'd put 'cooking' on mine. Abbey's given up these days. When we first met, she was an amazing cook. She was even on *Hell's Kitchen* cooking fancy food with proper chefs, and she'd put together the most amazing meals that had me salivating all the way back from the training ground. I'd rush back as fast as I could, and as I walked up the stairs I felt like the Bisto kid, sniffing the aroma of a freshly cooked shepherd's pie.

Abbey: I do love cooking, but with four kids coming and going all the time it became a chore and a thankless task. No matter what I cooked, everyone would have an opinion. *I don't like that anymore. I'm not eating that*. It's the last thing you want to hear when you've been slaving over a hot stove. For a while I considered making separate meals for us and the kids, but that's more work than anyone needs to put food on the table for the family. If I make something and everyone likes it, I'll make it again and again. If it doesn't go down well, I won't bother again. It's funny how quickly your repertoire of meals gets smaller when you think like that. So there are times when I wish Pete's prowess at the barbecue or in the kitchen was a little more finely tuned.

Peter: From time to time, though, Abbey goes full-on Nigella. She reserves these moments of gastronomic genius for when she's trying to get me off the golf course. I know what she's doing. I've totally rumbled her. But still ... I just can't resist it. She'll send me photos of marinating lamb chops just as I'm teeing off. She'll add a cheeky little text: 'Supper's nearly ready.' And even if I manage to ignore that opening salvo, she'll follow it up with a barrage of updates at each stage of the cooking process. It's just too much. I'll be salivating by the third hole. She gets into my head, stops me focusing. All I can think about is lamb chops. And if I still manage to resist, she'll play her ace card: a suggestive beaver emoji. At that point I'll be chucking the clubs in the car and legging it home.

Abbey: Guilty as charged. It's a blatant ploy to get him home in time for supper. Otherwise he'd be on the golf course all evening. He hasn't twigged that if he brushed up on his barbecuing skills he'd be able to sizzle his own lamb chops whenever he wanted, but I don't think we'll tell him that, shall we?

Q is for Queen

There are two people in the world who famously don't carry money: Her Late Majesty Queen Elizabeth II, and Abbey ...

Peter: But where the Queen had a host of butlers and flunkies to carry her bits and bobs, Abbey has me.

Like the Queen, she never leaves the house with a bank card or a key. For someone so organised, it flabbergasts me. When she parks her car, she takes a picture of the meter and sends it to me so I can pay for the parking online. The Queen would never have had RingGo on her phone, so why should Abbey?

In fairness, there have been times when she has deigned to slum it like us commoners and take a bank card with her. But I've never known a person with such a flagrant disregard for these cards. I couldn't begin to tell you how many we've been through as a couple, because once she's lost all hers, she'll start making inroads on mine. And if I lend her my bank card, it's a nailed-on certainty that she'll lose it within half an hour.

Abbey: I don't know how it happens. It's like I'm surrounded by some kind of magical bank-card black hole. Every time I have a card in my hand – especially if it's one of Pete's – it turns into a comedy sketch. I can lose bank cards in places where it's impossible to lose anything. It's a bit of a talent. I was once sitting having my hair done when Pete gave me his card so I could pay for something on my phone. I didn't even move from my chair, and even then, somehow the card simply vanished. It would be impressive if it wasn't dead embarrassing.

Peter: I'm a mild man. It takes a lot to rile me. I'm not prone to expressions of fury, but it's reached the stage where even I get a little bit angry. I've had to start hiding my bank cards from her, banning her from ever borrowing them.

Abbey: I had Pete's bank card in my back pocket once, and I'd just had a proper telling-off for losing the last one. Sure enough, I was out at the shops and I reached for it, only to find that it was gone. Nightmare. I was seriously panicking, shaking like a teenager terrified of fessing up to their parents for raiding the drinks cabinet with their mates, trying to retrace my steps to find the bloody little bit of plastic before Pete found out I'd lost it. No chance. Pete sent me a text with a picture: his bank card, bent out of shape, perfectly moulded to the shape of my arse.

Peter: And retrieved from under the stool in our bedroom.

Abbey: We did come up with a solution for this problem: Apple Pay. If anything has improved our marriage, it's Apple Pay. But it's not foolproof, because half the time I don't have charge on my phone, so Pete will have to follow me into a shop at a respectful distance, and when the time comes to settle up, he'll have to come and take care of business.

Peter: Just like one of the Queen's flunkies. And that's just the way it is: she's Her Majesty, and I'm the Paul Burrell of the footballing world.

R

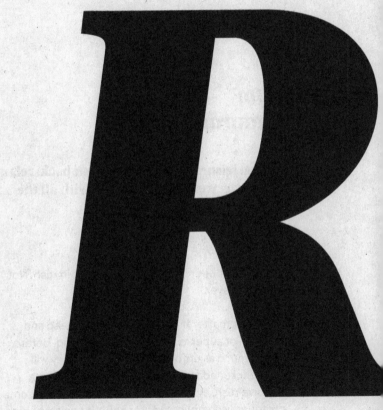

R is for *estaurant Rush*

A long, leisurely meal. Time to sit back, relax and graze over several courses with all the time in the world.

Er, no thanks ...

Peter: We've never been into a restaurant not in rush. Not once. Not ever.

It doesn't matter if we're somewhere cheap and cheerful or super-posh. We'll sit down and, before I've so much as unfolded my napkin, Abbey will have beckoned the waiter over to say we're in a massive rush, even if we're not. She'll make up some profoundly complicated story about having to pick up the kids in 20 minutes, or only having 40 minutes left on the parking meter. There I am, expecting a nice leisurely lunch, wide-eyed as I listen aghast to the torrent of lies pouring from Abbey's mouth.

Next up, she'll take a quick look at her menu and order before the waiter has even had a chance to hand me mine. My bum has barely made contact with the chair and she has seized control. There's not much point me even opening my menu, because Abbey will have ordered for me, like I'm a little kid. She'll snap her menu shut and remind the waiter that we've only got 19 minutes left now. Somewhere in the back of my mind I can hear the seconds ticking down on the *Countdown* clock.

Abbey: I can't bear waiting for food. I have to eat straight away – partly because I'm hungry, but mostly because I hate sitting around. The menu might be full of rich ragus, melt-in-the-mouth slow-cooked beef and triple-cooked chips, and it all sounds delicious, but if it can't be in front of me within five minutes of ordering, I'm not interested. Speed over taste, every time. Whatever comes quickest out of the kitchen is the right meal for me, even if there's something tastier to be had.

Peter: Abbey has to eat something literally the moment her eyes ping open, which is why she does such excellent justice to a hotel buffet breakfast. You can set your clock by her hunger, which is why the restaurant rush is such a thing.

We have tried to change our eating habits in the past. We once watched a documentary on Netflix called *What the Health*, and it had such a profound effect on us that we decided to go vegan. It was quite a challenge for such a carnivorous family. We spent two weeks eating a diet of brown rice and falafels. And then something else had a profound effect on us: the golden arches of the McDonald's sign appearing like a mirage to a thirsty traveller as we drove along the motorway. It was a moment of divine intervention. We followed that golden sign like the three kings following the star. Right there and then we decided to call an end to our family vegan experiment. And what better way to celebrate than with a Big Mac? Meaty, delicious and – if you're in a restaurant rush – *fast* ...

R is for Romantic Date Nights

Date night: a chance to get all dressed up and gaze lovingly into each other's eyes as you remember that you do rather like each other after all. But after 17 years and four kids, can you really be bothered?

Abbey: I'm not saying I want to be a man. But the only time I *would* want to be a man is when I think about romantic date nights. And that's because I would be a *far* better romantic man than Pete ever will be.

Peter: That's because you know what women want from a date. It's such a complex game, with infinite subtleties, and we men are very simple creatures.

Abbey: It's really not that hard to be romantic. All you have to do is watch a romcom if you've run out of ideas. Any of them would be better than our infamous TomTom date. It happened around the time I suspected Peter had bought the engagement ring. He'd also very romantically bought me a TomTom – this was in the days before every phone had a satnav – and suggested we took it out for a ride. I got done up to death thinking he was going to propose to me. He would set the TomTom to direct us to somewhere breathtakingly romantic, then he'd get down on one knee and pop the question.

But no, he actually was just testing the TomTom.

It's so easy to impress a woman with little romantic gestures. Pete doesn't seem to realise he could get away with murder if he only made a bit more of an effort.

Peter: I do *sometimes* make an effort. What about the time I took you to a hotel and you had no idea where we were going, and I'd packed an outfit for you? The whole shebang: dress, shoes, bag. Restaurant booked, nothing for you to think about. Don't tell me that wasn't romantic.

Abbey: It *was* romantic. It was also 15 years ago. So while it might have been a good gesture, it didn't give you enough credit in the bank to last 15 years.

Peter: So what about the time I took you out on a little dinghy off the coast of Sardinia. Just you, me, a picnic and a bottle of champagne. We pulled anchor in the middle of nowhere, cracked open the champers ...

Abbey: That *was* very romantic – right up until the point that the wind changed, the anchor got stuck and we almost died when another boat hit us.

The time you booked a chef to cook us dinner at home was very romantic too, or would have been if the chef hadn't sat with us the whole time and kind of killed the vibe, and then we just went to bed and watched Netflix.

Peter: What I don't understand is this: why is it always the man who has to make the big romantic gestures? We also like to be wined and dined and whisked off to Paris.

Abbey: I *would* whisk you off to Paris, if I wasn't completely certain that if you had a spare three days you'd much rather be playing golf.

To be fair, it's not always easy. We went through a phase of booking dinners and cinema tickets for date nights when the kids were babies. We'd book something every week, and we'd look forward to it. And then, regular as clockwork, every week we'd cancel it. An 8pm movie? By the time all the children were in bed, we were so bloody tired all we wanted to do was go to bed ourselves and conk out. We'd get to 7.30, look at each other and say, 'Sod it.'

We tried so many times to have those date nights, but eventually we just gave up. Now, a date for us is more likely to consist of sitting down to have a glass of wine and a chat once the kids are in bed. A single glass of Chardonnay and we're tucked up by 8.30. Bliss!

Peter: It is important to make time for each other, though. Otherwise all you end up doing is getting through the day and not enjoying it. It's so easy to get wrapped up in work and family life when you've been together for a long time. Every now and then, when we do manage a night out or, even better, a night away, it's so much fun. We laugh so much. We're just us, a couple instead of Mum and Dad, and we always come away remembering that we do actually like each other after all.

Our real problem, though, is that nobody really wants to mind four kids on their own. It seemed to be OK when there were only three of them, but four seems to be the tipping point. Sometimes Abbey's mum comes round to look after them, but it's a lot for one person. We've sometimes resorted to having two babysitters so that they can divide and conquer. Two babysitters, just to go and see *Barbie*! By the time you've paid for that and the tickets, you've gone right off the idea.

Abbey: You're already a hundred quid down before you've even had a sniff of sangria. Frankly, it's easier to stay at home and order a curry!

R is for Routine

The bedtime routine. It should be calm and relaxing, a gentle end to a busy day and a pleasant prelude to a good night's sleep.

It *should* be that, but somehow it isn't ...

Abbey: A bedtime routine is supposed to make your life easier. Ours does the exact opposite. Getting Liberty, Jack and Johnny to bed is a process that used to take an hour and now takes all sodding evening. All because Pete made the mistake of inventing a game called Catch in the Bath.

And yes, it all starts with bathtime. That's when the bedlam kicks in, because we have to try to catch them and put them in the bath. Off they run around the house to evade capture. It's harder than marking Ronaldo. We have to catch each one individually and put them in the bath before turning our attention to the next. I'm not exaggerating when I say it takes us hours. It's like herding cats: just as you have one, another slips through your fingers and heads straight back downstairs, so you have to start all over again.

Peter: It's totally my fault. I invented the game a few years ago, but now they've had so much practice that they're brilliant at it – so little and fast. When you catch one, they beg to be released for another chance. As soon as we gave in once, that became part of the routine too. They scream and shout and don't want to be caught first, so now we have to bribe Liberty to let us catch her. Once she's been caught, it's easier to tempt the boys to bed when they know they've outlasted their sister.

Abbey: Supernanny would definitely say we are doing everything wrong. She'd tell us we should have a hard-and-fast lights-out time, and that nobody should be allowed to leave their bedroom. But let's face it, at the end of the day, bedtime is all about survival. The end is in sight, you imagine yourself sinking into the sofa for a bit of peaceful time in the tiny bit of the evening that's left, and you do what you have to do to get there …

Peter: The bedtime routine was much easier with one child. You'd lie down with them, read a book and soon they'd be asleep. Now it's bedlam. They play tag team through the night, running in and out of different rooms, playing musical beds and making sure Mum and Dad don't get any sleep.

Abbey: The boys used to have car-shaped beds. I thought it would be a great idea – if they thought they were in a Maserati, maybe they'd never leave. That backfired too. Whenever one of them needed settling, Pete would climb into the Maserati to reassure them. More often than not, he'd drift off to sleep, hoping the boys would follow his lead. But once he was asleep, they'd creep out of bed and come to sleep with me. It meant Pete was spending more time in the Maserati than the boys. As it was half the size of a normal bed, he'd unfurl himself in the morning and be in agony. He ended up with chronic back pain and under the care of a chiropractor.

Peter: At least the Maserati was better than the princess-carriage bed. That really was unbearable. I'd wake up in such a bad mood after a night of being Cinderella, especially as princess beds really aren't designed for six-foot-seven blokes who need room for their feet to hang off the end.

Abbey: Even now, the boys come into our bed almost every night, and it's always Pete who gets kicked out. He knows his place. We even had a single mattress on the floor for the best part of a year, where Pete would sleep while the kids joined me for the best spot in the house. I don't mind. They're so sweet and soft to hold in your arms. I know it won't last for ever, so I'm not in any massive hurry to kick them out of bed. Pete is!

Peter: Too right. I've spent enough nights on that mattress curled up like the dog. It's no wonder he responds to me so well. With our crazy night-time routine, he must see me as one of the pack.

S

S *is for* *ex*

'Dear Peter and Abbey, what's your advice for keeping the spark alive once you start to hear the patter of tiny feet?'

Abbey: All I'm going to say about sex is this: Pete can send all the beaver emojis he wants, there's nothing like four children, an endless stream of builders and handymen, and the constant presence of my brother staying for months at a time to cool the libido a little.

Peter: When we built our house, Abbey and I said we'd go round the whole place and christen each room. In eight years we've managed two rooms, and one of those is our bedroom. I'm not going to tell you which the other room is, but perhaps by the time I'm 60 we'll have made it round the whole of the ground floor.

S is for Social Media

Scroll through Instagram and you'd be forgiven for thinking that everyone else is glamorous and popular and living their best lives, while you're sitting on the sofa eating Rich Teas. Don't believe a word of it ...

Abbey: We both spend a lot of time on social media, but that doesn't mean we don't worry about its problems and pitfalls. Nobody looks as good in the flesh as they do on social media, and there are so many tricks and filters people use to make themselves appear better. Even if you know that, scrolling through Instagram can still make you feel really rubbish. Twitter isn't much better – everyone seems so angry there, and you're only one tweet away from being cancelled. TikTok is a rabbit hole. You can lose hours of your life to it, and only come away with a new dance routine to show for it.

I particularly worry about what it's doing to our kids. When we were 18, there was no lasting evidence of what we got up to or our inevitable mistakes. OK, maybe there was a pack of Snappy Snaps pictures showing us all orange with shit hair extensions, but you could easily relegate that to the back of your sock drawer. Now, put a dodgy photo online and the whole world can see it.

Our children have never had more access to the world, and the world, in turn, has never had such access to them. You can't protect them from everything out there, so instead I want my children to know that if they ever see something worrying, they can always talk about it. I live in fear of some creep befriending one of the kids, so I'm forever warning them that they should only add someone on Instagram if they definitely know them. There's a part of me that wants to stop them having access to any of it, but you don't want your child to be the odd one out.

Peter: That's definitely true. You can't feel like you're missing out on stuff. If you don't have social media and messaging services, you won't know about anything, because nobody talks to each other on the phone anymore. But it's a challenge. When we were young, you'd come home from school and kick a ball about with your mates in the street, and you wouldn't speak to your classmates again until you walked into school the next day. Now you're online and on show all the time.

Abbey: We do try to have rules in our house about phones and access to computers, but it doesn't help that Pete and I are so computer illiterate. We can't even use Find My iPhone, let alone block content or tweak everyone's internet access settings. But what I do know is that social media is just the tip of the technology iceberg. Pete will say that I'm on my phone a lot, which is true, but in my defence I'm usually looking for tips on how to grow vegetables for the day I finally have my kitchen garden and an abundance of homegrown carrots and lettuce, so it feels like a healthy pursuit. YouTube, though? That's a beast, because it's apparently bottomless. When we were little, we'd be allowed to watch an episode of our favourite programme if it happened to be on, but it was easy for our parents to turn off the TV because there was nothing else to watch. Now a kid's favourite programme can be on an endless loop for hours and hours. It's impossible to tear them away from the screen because they want Just One More!

Peter: So do we fess up about the *Peppa Pig* fiasco?

Abbey: Don't even talk to me about *Peppa Pig*.

Peter: We were on holiday in Dubai when Sophia was a baby. Abbey was letting her watch *Peppa Pig* on the phone. Quite a lot. I mean, we try to be the best parents we can. It's a bit tragic when you see families on holiday, all sitting around the meal table staring at their phones without talking to the people they're with. But sometimes you're exhausted and can't help but resort to the electronic babysitter for a moment's peace. We failed to take into account the data-roaming charges. I don't even want to think about the size of that phone bill. Thousands of pounds. Most expensive babysitter ever!

T

T *is for allness*

He's big, he's red, his feet stick out the bed. But let's not go on about it.

Peter: Beanpole. Lanky. Freak. Twenty-foot chicken. A biological experiment gone wrong. You name it, I've been called it. I've been mocked in the press and booed by my own fans. After signing for QPR, I walked out on to the pitch and heard laughter in the stands. Don't ask me why. It's not as if I can do anything about my height. I can't change it, so I don't understand why people say such personal things. I've always tried to rise above it, though, to make myself a stronger and more resilient person.

Aside from the bullying, the worst thing about my height is finding clothes that fit. Most trousers stop halfway up my legs. Sometimes I have to resort to having things made for me – not cheap.

Abbey: Only now we've found a magic website to solve these problems.

Peter: 2tall.com. Lifesaver. I find it funny to see who follows them on social media: Stephen Merchant, Vernon Kay, Dan Walker – all the tall tribe. Another clothes place for us tall chaps is called High and Mighty. My problem is that, although I *am* high, I'm not all that mighty: the waists are always too big and the jackets enormous. People assume that if you're tall, you're large, and I'm not.

Abbey: Our children are tall too. They came out tiny but within a month they were a chip off the old block. What you notice as the mother of tall children is that everyone thinks they have a right to comment on their height. It's a problem exclusive to the tall. Nobody says, 'Hi, shorty! Have you forgotten to take your vitamins?' Nobody says, 'Look at the blubber on him! How big is her arse?' But people happily say, 'Oh my God, how tall is he? How's the oxygen up there?'

Peter: If you're *reasonably* tall, it's considered cool. 'Isn't he tall! Hasn't he grown?!' But if you're *too* tall, it isn't. I don't know what the cut-off height is. I don't know how tall is too tall.

Abbey: But I do know that Pete was too tall for Glastonbury. He came out of the blocks too strong on the first day and had too many beers, too many shots and far too much fun, like a Brit tourist who overcooks on the first night on holiday. He was like a drunk giraffe. The weight of his folded-over body was too much for me. I couldn't carry him or drag him anywhere, so he was just slumped on top of me, all arms and legs. He ruined my Glastonbury by being too tall and too drunk.

Peter: Too many arms, too many legs, too many beers – it's a bad combo!

It used to be only the tall girls who'd give me a second glance. Our eyes would meet – over everyone else's heads, naturally – and she'd look at me and think, *Finally – someone taller than me!* But I read somewhere that tall blokes are genetically programmed to like short women. It's as if nature is sorting out the gene pool.

I've only ever encountered a couple of people taller than me, and it was really unnerving. I met one fellow who was seven-foot-five. It was discombobulating having to crane my neck up to talk to him. I never normally have to look up. I'm usually hunched over people, and I have to be careful where I stand in photographs.

Abbey: At the back, in the middle, obviously.

Peter: I know my place.

T is for attoos

Tattoos and footballers go together like footballers and golf.

With one exception ...

Peter: These days it seems like every single footballer who has ever so much as sat on a bench in League Two has a tat. They're so commonplace you'd think it was written into the contract that you have to have one. And they don't just have tiny, subtle tats with the initials of their children. They have a whole sleeve, from wrist to neck. One minute they're coming up through the youth system, the next they have a full multicolour T-shirt made out of ink. Every single footballer has them.

Except me, for two reasons.

This first reason is that a tattoo all the way up my arm would make a serious dent in the world's ink supplies. The second is that most tattoos remind me of the scribbles you'd find on a school desk, or worse, on the walls of a cubicle in a service station on the M62.

Abbey: And then there are the fans who get pictures of their favourite player tattooed onto their body. I'm not sure what happens when they transfer to a new club. One bloke once threatened to have Pete's arse tattooed on his face. Surely he meant Pete's face on his arse? I can sensationally reveal that Pete's arse is not all that distinctive, and I'm really not sure how this bloke would know what it looks like anyway. Maybe it's some trend that we are both entirely unaware of ...

Peter: Getting a tattoo just never, ever crossed my mind. I never wanted to draw attention to my long arms and legs. I suppose I could get quite a bit of writing down my thigh, though. A novel, perhaps. Maybe *War and Peace*. Or I could list every club I ever played for – you'd need a long limb for that.

But I don't think I could be bothered with it. Tattoos seem like such a pain to look after. The showers after a game would be full of stark-naked blokes with their arms wrapped in cling film to avoid getting their new artwork wet. Then they'd have to rub the thing with cream. What a load of shit for a load of shit ...

Tattoo addiction is definitely a thing. Nobody ever has just one. One leads to two, two to three, and so on. They breed. Before you know it, you're covered. The irony is that they're supposed to be rebellious, but now that everyone's covered in tats, it's more edgy and cool if you're *not* in the shower covered in cling film and clutching a massive pot of moisturiser.

David Beckham has a lot to answer for. He inspired the footballing tattoo epidemic, especially the neck and hand tattoo that had previously been the sole preserve of the serial killer. David also famously got his wife's name tattooed in Sanskrit, but the tattooist made a spelling mistake. 'Vihctoria' doesn't have quite the same ring to it, but at least there aren't many Sanskrit-speaking footy fans, so he just about got away with it.

Abbey: I have quite freckly pale skin, which I don't think would suit a tattoo. If I had olive skin I might think about it, but I've lived this long without one, so I think it would be a bit strange to go down that path now.

And I don't think I really have the tattoo mentality. My brother has a flying prawn tattooed on his arm. He explained his reasoning: 'I love prawns. And that's a flying prawn. So it means live your life and follow your dreams.' Now, I like a *gambas pil pil* as much as the next person, but I really don't think I want a plate of them tattooed on my arm.

Peter: A mate of mine had his own birthday tattooed on his arm. It's 9 October, but the tattooist got it wrong and now he's walking around with a giant '9/11' on his arm. I'm not sure it's the look he was after. I think I'll stick to writing birthdays down in my calendar rather than having them etched onto my own skin.

At the end of the day, I think it's fine to have your kids' names on your football boots, but I draw the line at having them engraved on my arse. It's hardly the perfect reminder. 'What's his name, that ginger one I've loved and cherished for the last ten years? Have a look at my arse and tell me, would you?'

Agony ~~Aunt~~ Ab

Dear Abbey,

Please help! Every time I get a new boyfriend my big brothers manage to put them off. I can confirm they have officially lost me four out of five proper boyfriends.

My current boyfriend's name is Richard Acorn, so of course they've started calling him Acorn Dick.

The jokes have persisted relentlessly for a good six months now. One night, Rich had had enough and said, 'I bet mine is bigger than yours!' My brother reacted with 'Go on, then, let's see it,' and they proceeded to have a dick-off.

The whole family got involved, making bets as my soul left my body. I've never been more embarrassed.

I thought this was going to be the worst moment of my life, but that came when, sadly, my little bro's penis was, at that moment, larger than my boyfriend's.

And so the names keep coming. Conker Cock has been another. I actually cannot repeat the rest – they just get worse and worse. I really like Rich, but my family make it so difficult for us and they can't seem to accept him.

How can I help Rich get his own back on my two brothers, who are both complete melts in their own right? More importantly, how does Rich secure his place in the family? I hate being single, and I think Rich might well be the one.

Stacey, 23 – Leeds

Abbey: I feel for you Stacey and Acorn Dick. I come from a large Scouse family and there's always lots of banter floating about. It can be quite intimidating.

Peter: I grew up in football changing rooms so banter and name calling is definitely something I am used to too. I can usually hold my own but this scenario is particularly horrendous.

Abbey: What an unfortunate name Richard Acorn is.

Peter: I've heard about someone called Richard Brie who is always being called Dick Cheese so it could be worse.

Abbey: As the oldest of four I am very protective of my siblings. In the past when they have brought home new girlfriends and boyfriends, it's been like something from *Meet the Fockers* with the circle of trust.

We make it clear that they need to earn their place in the family. We'll vet new partners and push them to the limits and only when they have conquered the assault course of abuse and ridicule are they allowed in.

Peter: Woe betide when our daughters are older and they bring someone home, Richard Acorn is getting nothing in comparison to the stick I'll give the girls' partners.

Abbey: Stacey, I think if your partner can survive getting his penis out in front of your family, being ridiculed for the size of it and *still* he is sticking around, then he is a keeper.

U

U is for Underwear

Abbey is a Victoria's Secret model, so lacy knickers go with the territory. But even underwear models are partial to wearing the occasional pair of granny pants.

Abbey: I am a full-blown, unapologetic underwear snob. I like the good stuff. I wear beautiful matching underwear every day because I think it makes a difference to how you feel about yourself. If you're wearing something fabulous, you feel fabulous. That sensational silky underwear gives you a boost you can't get anywhere else.

But that doesn't mean I don't also have a stash of flesh-coloured knickers, which Pete absolutely hates.

Peter: I haven't even seen the flesh-coloured knickers for years. I rarely get underneath the dressing gown these days. Abbey double-knots her dressing gown: one knot at the front, one at the back. It's like Fort Knox. It's like it's been tied by a ninja.

Abbey: And for good reason. One of my pet hates is when I've had a shower and I'm getting ready, applying my make-up and doing my hair, and Pete comes in and puts his hands all over me. I'm usually in a rush, feeling hot and bothered and hoping to get out of the house on time without precipitating some disastrous four-child incident. The last thing I need is filthy paws all over my silky drawers, as someone once said.

Peter: You can't blame a man for trying. But there's no way I'm getting into that dressing gown when Abs is getting ready. I'm not Harry Houdini. Although I have noticed that the double Fort Knox ninja knot is quite often tied even when she's staying at home. Maybe it's just to hide the flesh-coloured knickers. Yeah, that's probably it.

V

V is for *alentines*

Everything stops for Valentine's Day. It's the law. At least, that's what Pete and Abbey tell the kids ...

Peter: I like Valentine's Day. When else do you have the perfect excuse to do something together without the kids? 'Sorry, Mummy and Daddy absolutely *have* to go out tonight. It's the law that you have to go out on Valentine's Day.' That said, I do like to get the children involved. I always think of it as a day to treat Abbey, so I get them to make the cards while I sort out the flowers before taking her out to dinner.

Abbey: He's quite romantic, really. I've already mentioned how, when we first got together, he used to write me poems and cards. He doesn't quite go that far anymore, but he still pulls out the stops for Valentine's Day.

Peter: Last year we went to a restaurant in London and happened to bump into a group of friends. Unbelievably, they'd chosen the same restaurant. Who'd have thought it? The restaurant also had a casino, so we had a lovely dinner then went down to the casino with them all. It might not have been the most romantic night out, but we had such a lot of fun that we forgot to cash in our chips at the end of the night. Who said you can't put a price on romance?

V is for *irgin*

Losing your virginity is one of those milestones in life. A magical moment as the earth moves and two become one. Also, the basis of an excellent chat-show gag.

Peter: I was once asked in an interview with Graham Norton what I would be if I hadn't been a footballer. The answer just dropped into my head. I didn't pause, not even for a single beat: 'A virgin.' It was over 15 years ago and that gag has followed me round ever since. Can't complain, though, because it's probably true!

Abbey: Bless. Maybe I should have it engraved on your tombstone if you go before me.

W

W is for Weddings

It's the happiest day of anyone's life. A day to celebrate the love a couple shares before sending them on their way to a lifetime of joy and constant bliss.

But they're not always plain sailing ...

Abbey: Our first wedding was cancelled. We'd planned to get married in Italy, and the whole day was planned. An amazing hotel where all our guests would stay. The wedding itself on a tiny private island on a magical Italian lake. Traditional Italian food, fine wines, a classical orchestra ... We'd organised it all down to the tiniest detail, and then, a month before we were due to fly a hundred guests out there, the flights were cancelled. What had been shaping up to be a dream became a total nightmare. Since I was pregnant at the time, we decided to cancel the whole thing.

Wedding Mark II took place at Stapleford Park, near Melton Mowbray in Leicestershire, home of those little pork pies you have at picnics. By that time I'd given birth to Sophia, who was three months old. We were so obsessed with our beautiful new baby and had to do things a little differently. Everyone was amazing and rallied around. Giles Deacon, who designed my dress, had the dress delivered straight from his studio in a lorry containing only a single mannequin with my handmade gown beautifully displayed on it, the train all laid out the full length of the lorry. What a sight it was to see!

I might have been preoccupied with being a new mum in the run-up, but we still had the most amazing day. Everybody who was there says it was the best wedding they've been to, even after all these years. It wasn't without the usual hiccups, though. Drama with the bridesmaids' dresses? Tick. Tension with the mother-in-law? Tick. I was far too tired after having Sophia to turn into a Bridezilla, though. I did, however, perhaps go a teensy bit over the top in my plans for looking after her for the day.

Peter: A teensy bit? Sophia had more security than the President of the United States.

Abbey: My whole family was obviously coming to the wedding, which meant all the people I would usually have trusted to look after Sophia were spoken for and I didn't have anyone to babysit my precious first child. The hotel kindly supplied a nanny, but I was scared to leave the baby with a nanny I didn't know, so I hired a security guard to watch her.

But my paranoid new-mum brain wasn't satisfied. What if the nanny and the security guard conspired to kidnap Sophia? I couldn't let that happen, so I hired a second security guard to watch the first security guard who was watching the nanny.

Peter: What a totally normal and sane response. And what a lovely moment it was when, at the end of the reception, I carried Abbey over the threshold into the honeymoon suite, only to find the room full of people: a security guard watching another security guard watching a nanny watching a baby, who was fast asleep, all wrapped up in a blanket, her eyes firmly shut. I'd completely forgotten they'd be there, and it frightened the crap out of me!

Abbey: A fitting end to a day that had begun chaotically. We'd abided by tradition in not spending the night before together. I'd gone to bed early in the coach house separate from the main hotel, wanting to get my beauty sleep so I could look my best for my husband in the morning. My sleep was broken by a commotion outside my room. It was light outside, and Peter, my brother, my cousin and two of his friends were fooling around on the lawn wearing their suits. Panic! I'd overslept! Then I looked at the time. It was 5.30am. They hadn't even been to bed, the absolute bastards.

Peter: I'd been holding the fort in the main hotel. Each time a guest arrived, they wanted to have a beer with me. Then the family arrived, and they *definitely* wanted to have a beer with me. What else was I supposed to do?

Abbey: The day didn't get easier. The make-up artist crashed on the motorway. She wasn't hurt, thank goodness, but she couldn't get to me, so I had to do my own make-up. I wanted to feel like me so I had smokey eyes and red nail varnish. I'd had amazing long hair extensions put in especially for the wedding but the hairdresser cut them out on the day. Thankfully when I put my wedding dress on, it fitted me perfectly and I felt like a million dollars.

Peter: The whole day was reassuringly expensive. We had a wedding planner, and I'm certain they saw us coming and added a zero to everything. The bill for the flowers was enough to keep a small country afloat (yes, chaps, apparently you do need them at a wedding). I thought about ditching the cake because, really, what's the point of it? Nobody eats the stuff. It's just so you can have the 'moment' of cutting it, but I can think of plenty of moments we could have for that sort of cash.

Abbey: At some point, somebody – probably the wedding planner, because it sure as hell wasn't me – had suggested that we have a harp-playing child singing 'You Are So Beautiful' as I walked up the aisle. We walked into the reception to Nicki Minaj singing 'Moment 4 Life'. Who were we?

Peter: Harp-playing children? Nicki Minaj?

Looking back now at some of the things we planned, it was all a bit outrageous and not very us. We thought that because I was a footballer, we had to do the things footballers do, even though we didn't really want them. It was fashionable at the time to have famous music artists playing at footballers' weddings. Wayne Rooney had booked the Stereophonics. I looked into hiring Simply Red, but they cost a million quid. No thanks. We ended up with Beverley Knight, who was a friend of a friend. She was wonderful, talented and it was great to have her. So it does, in retrospect, feel like a slightly mad thing to have done. A bit like the ridiculous boiled-egg dessert Abbey ordered.

Abbey: It was an eggshell, with a mango yolk and a meringue for the egg white. All very Heston Blumenthal. We even had a giant vodka luge ...

Peter: A wedding planner told me once that when it comes to spending a lot of money at a wedding you can burn it (fireworks) or melt it (ice sculptures). We burned it *and* melted it, as we had fireworks too.

Abbey: Every time I went to the loo, I had to get completely naked because the dress wouldn't fit in the bloody cubicle. The whole thing had to come off.

Peter: Sadly, I wasn't there to witness that.

Abbey: All in all, our wedding was incredible, spectacular but pretty bonkers, but I see weddings on Instagram these days that are even more outrageous. A child playing the harp and a novelty egg dessert are nothing compared to the ice chandeliers and clouds of white rose petals that seem to be de rigueur. I think the whole thing has grown completely out of proportion. Looking back, running off into the sunset together and not having to deal with any of the planning might have been more us. That would be my advice to any young bride now: ditch the big wedding, save your cash and do something simple.

Recently we renewed our vows. It was a lot simpler than our real wedding and all the better for it. We went to the Maldives together as a family and brought some friends with us. It was magical. We all wore white and danced into the night.

W is for WhatsApp Groups

Nothing can prepare you for the relentless horror of the class WhatsApp group. The endless pinging. The incessant messages. The off-colour memes from Abbey Clancy ...

Peter: I would rather Abbey served me with divorce papers than added me to the school WhatsApp groups. She threatens to do it when I'm not across the admin or aware of the kids' social arrangements (which is, admittedly, most of the time). What I hear about these groups is enough to put me off for life.

Abbey: I'm desperate to leave the WhatsApp groups too, but they're the only way you can keep up with everything that's going on. It means you're relentlessly bombarded with messages about uniform, after-school clubs, trips, homework instructions, end-of-year presents for the teacher, discos ... Every day there's something new to contend with, and I have it four times over with things to remember for each child.

The worst aspect of these groups is when people feel the need to reply even when they have nothing to say. If someone posts, 'Elijah is missing his games top, does anyone have it?' it is *not necessary* for every parent who *hasn't* got it to reply, 'No,' with a sad-face emoji. You put your phone down for an hour, and before you know it you have to sift through a hundred messages, because somewhere buried deep is an important message saying that school finishes early the next day.

I caused chaos when I suggested we have two groups: one for announcements, which nobody should reply to, and one for general chat, which we could mute if we wanted. My smart-arse idea completely backfired, because now I have eight groups to contend with instead of four.

It's not just the big class-wide groups that cause me grief, either. There are small groups of just a few parents, and I almost got kicked out of one of those the other day. I shared a silly meme, which may or may not have included a picture of a man with his penis out. Big mistake. I thought it was funny, but Pete told me it was the wrong audience for the joke and I should have listened. The school run was no fun the next day, as I had to grovel my apologies to everyone.

Peter: Abbey and I were out having some drinks one evening when she told me about a mums' group outing to the cinema. She said that if she wanted to meet up with a large group of women, she'd rather sit and have a crisp glass of white wine with them than go to see *Spider-Man 3*. So I persuaded her to put on the WhatsApp group that she couldn't join them, as we were going to David and Elton's party. We weren't. There was no party. But we figured that everyone in the group thought we were a bunch of arses anyway, so why not? We were in a tapas bar in Weybridge on our fourth sangria, crying with laughter. (I thought putting David before Elton was particularly choice ...)

Abbey: I think I'd reached peak group by that time. I'm part of so many of them where people are whinging about whether the school meals are healthy enough or asking which PE kit they need the next day. It was driving me mad. I had to throw something in there to put the cat among the pigeons.

Peter: It's not just the school groups that have got out of hand. There's a group for everything these days. You go away for a weekend with some mates in Cornwall, and suddenly 'Team Cornwall' is pinging away on your bloody phone every two minutes. You're probably in another group with exactly the same people already, but you can't leave this one, and so the vicious circle of WhatsApp groups continues.

My favourite thing about WhatsApp groups, though, is when someone leaves. There's something wonderfully passive-aggressive about the announcement 'John has left the group'. What did we do, John? We had fun on holiday, didn't we? Is it over now between us, John? It feels like a WhatsApp mic drop.

It should be more socially acceptable to mute the thing and sit there on the sidelines observing. My entire WhatsApp is muted. In fact, my whole phone is muted. The downside is that when I lose it and try calling it, I can't hear it ring. The upside is that I can catch up on three whole days' worth of messages in two minutes, rather than jumping every single time the damn thing pings. Half the time you don't need to respond anyway.

Abbey: I think you'll find you don't need to respond *most* of the time.

W is for Wine

Peter and Abbey are quite partial to a glass of something after a long, hard day. Red? White? Pink? Bubbles? Who cares, as long as it's served in a large glass and doesn't come out a suspicious shade of brown.

Peter: There's a wall in my office where Abbey has hung all my England caps. Alongside them is a decent collection of giant bottles of champagne, awarded to me for being Man of the Match. I never opened any of them when I was a player. Recently we had friends over and they'd drunk us out of wine, so I thought, *To hell with it!* We have enough of them. I could spare just one. I ran into my office, thrilled that at last we were going to crack open one of those babies. Who cared if it was a little bit warm? Champagne is champagne!

Or so I thought.

I lined up the flutes on the counter, basking in the glory of having solved our booze problem. I cracked open the bottle and poured its golden contents. Only it wasn't golden. It was brown. Turns out it was full of warm Carlsberg. Bit of a disappointment, although the blokes didn't seem to mind too much. A drink's a drink, after all.

I like Carlsberg, but I *really* like wine. I just don't know enough about it. It's on my list of things to improve on (see also DIY, cooking and learning Portuguese), because it's a bit embarrassing to look at the wine list and not know where to begin. David Beckham is always posting photos of him having just polished off a £1,300 bottle of plonk, but just because I'm a novice it doesn't stop me spending a fortune on wine. I just spend a fortune on wine I know nothing about.

Abbey: I love wine too. All the wines. Weirdly, I almost prefer petrol-station wine to the posh stuff. A bottle of Campino Classico from down the road slips down quite nicely, whereas the really expensive stuff makes me feel terrible the next day. I don't have a very strong constitution and some wines are just too heavy for me. I can't even look at a bottle of Châteauneuf du Pape, having vomited everywhere after a few glasses once, whereas Pete has to stay clear of the Whispering Angel.

Peter: They should call that stuff Shouting Devil. It gave me the worst hangover I've ever had after drinking it all day in the South of France. Now, I know that elsewhere in this book we've sung the praises of a well-managed hangover. But they aren't all like that. I'm an old geezer, I feel a lot worse in the morning than I did when I was 24 and could run flat out for 90 minutes without even thinking about it. That hangover was like nothing I've ever experienced. Abbey was in full-on nurse mode, putting a wet flannel on my forehead, and I was genuinely crying. I felt like I had a drill to the head. I had a cold can of Coke on each temple and I spent hours in bed, wailing. The pain was awful.

It's the day after that I hate. You open your eyes really slowly, hoping that maybe you might have got away with it. There's a sharp intake of breath and then the self-doubt kicks in. *What was I like? What did I say? Did I make a fool of myself?* It starts at the toes and then the wave of shame works its way up your body, accompanied by the palpitations, the shakes and the terrible tsunami of nausea.

Abbey: We joke about the bad side of drinking wine, but I genuinely love the role it plays in the Weekly Whine part of our podcast. Every week we share something that's bothered us about each other that week, then we say cheers and have a drink to put it to bed. I reckon that once we've finished this book we'll need a lot of wine to say cheers to all the whines we've shared!

W is for Working Together

They say don't ever work with animals or children. But what about working with your other half?

Abbey: I have older friends with kids in their twenties, which means they're able to do things as a couple. They might read the same book so they can discuss it. They might chat about the news without being constantly interrupted by the kids. They've even been on a six-week yoga course in India together. Which sounds kind of nice, doesn't it?

Now, don't get me wrong. I love my children with every bone in my body. But for years my life has revolved only around looking after them. They receive every last bit of my attention. We had so many children so close together that I lost touch with the rest of the world for a while.

That's why I love the fact that we've started our podcast. In all the years we've been together, we'd never worked together before until we took part in the Get Out Of My Ear segment on *Ant and Dec's Saturday Night Takeaway*. We loved doing that and when I made a few cameos on *That Peter Crouch Podcast*, it seemed to go down well. Where lockdown was a make or break moment for a lot of couples, we loved spending so much time together and the idea of working on a new podcast came up. I love working with Pete.

Peter: I love it too. It's a chance for some quality time, and who wouldn't want that? We have such a laugh recording our podcast, and I think laughter is one of the most vital ingredients in a relationship. So working together has been good for us. It's certainly a lot cheaper than going to couple's therapy!

Abbey: The title of the podcast is tongue and cheek but it is a bit like therapy for us, it's true. It's a chance for us to spend time talking to one another and I love that we get to reminisce about our relationship. It's not all roses, though. I sometimes worry about the Weekly Whine segment on the podcast, where we share what has wound us up about each other that week. Normally we don't really fight, so we have to sit there and think hard about what annoys us. Eventually I'll find something and then dwell on it. I worry that it makes me search for things to get wound up about that I'd never have noticed before.

Peter: Good point. If you think too hard about how I've annoyed you, if you talk about it and workshop it, all of a sudden you'll end up thinking ...

Abbey: Why the hell am I married to him?!

W is for Worrying

Some of us are life's worriers, anxious about every little thing. Some of us, on the other hand, are Peter Crouch.

Abbey: It's a real worry, how much I worry. I worry all the time, about everything. And then I worry about worrying all the time about everything. That's where Airport Abs comes from. What if *this* happens? What if *that* happens? What if something happens to one of the children? What if the plane falls out of the sky? What if we crash?

Most of all, though, I worry about health: my health and the health of those closest to me. It's constantly there, in my mind.

Peter: If one of us has a cough, it's throat cancer. A tight chest? It can only be lung cancer.

Abbey: I'm constantly googling my symptoms. I'll turn up at the doctors and announce that I have some obscure disease, and they'll look aghast and ask me how I know. And then as soon as they tell me I'm actually fine, the very real physical symptoms I was suffering from disappear completely. I should have married a doctor, really. Or, even better, I should have still married Pete but become a doctor myself.

I worry about having nice things when not everyone does. I worry that I should take everyone on holiday, because it's not fair that we can afford it and others can't. I worry about the kids and how they are getting on at school. It's quite a hindrance, and something I've had help for in the past. I have to watch myself, because otherwise it creeps back into my life and overwhelms me. And that's where I'm so grateful for Pete's calming influence.

Pete just shrugs things off and gets on with life. He's not at all anxious. I sometimes wonder if he's used up his lifetime quota of anxiety playing for England and trying to score for his clubs. The pressure on professional footballers is intense and they have to learn how to deal with it, otherwise they'd freeze at the big moments. You can't suddenly turn around and say, 'Nah, sorry, don't fancy it. Can Wayne have a go?'

Pete's resilient and tough. He was brought up that way. When he was a young boy at his first club, Spurs, his dad was so furious when Pete pulled out of a tackle that he left the game and Pete had to make his own way home. He never did it again. He's dedicated and focused. When all his schoolmates were off partying or travelling, he was working on his skills. That takes huge strength of character and it breeds resilience.

I think that if you can survive all of that with your sense of humour intact, if you can see it all off with that big laugh and hugely generous smile, nothing can really worry or touch you. And when you've been on the receiving end of the worst of people, you're never going to be fazed by losing your luggage at Faro Airport.

All this means that when something happens that might worry the rest of us, he asks himself, 'Can I do anything about it?' If the answer is no, why worry? What will be, will be. If it's out of your control, it shouldn't stay on your mind.

All in all, Pete's attitude balances things out a bit. We make a good team!

Peter: I do worry about *some* things. When I was playing, I was told what to do all the time. Everything was organised for me so I could just function on autopilot. Now that I'm my own boss I keep double-booking everything, and that stresses me out.

Abbey: What you're saying is, you worry about when you're going to fit in a game of golf.

Peter: Now that *does* worry me.

Agony ~~Aunt~~ Ab

Dear Abbey,

I'm fiercely independent, but when I'm with my man and we're out with his friends socialising, I'd like him to check in on me and make sure I am alright. He behaves completely differently when we are around his friends. When I speak to him about it, it falls on deaf ears. Even though we talk about it after nights out and he says he'll try harder next time, it doesn't happen. After a couple of drinks he becomes a lad, and it pisses me off. I don't want someone joined to my hip but just a little, 'Can I get you a drink, as I'm going up to the bar?' or, 'You OK, babe?' wouldn't go amiss.

I love my man and I know he loves me, but I need some help.

Anon.

Abbey: When we are on a night out, you are often to be found pretending to be a DJ in a DJ booth on stage somewhere, completely unaware of where I am.

Peter: I've only done that once. You don't say no if you get a chance to get up there with Groove Armada in Space in Ibiza. I've even got a great picture of me taken from behind as I look out at the crowd pretending to DJ. What an iconic moment that was.

I do always check in with you and ask if you want a drink or if you're having a good time, though. I'll keep coming back to you and seeing if you are OK.

If we're with your friends from school you won't check in on me, but when we're with my friends you keep coming near me and I'm like, 'Go away!'

I think Anon is justified in wanting this. It's nice to catch up with your friends, but you've got to make sure your girl is OK.

X

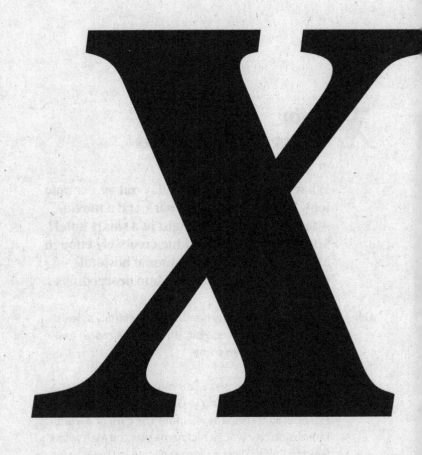

X is for *-rays and cocktails*

What would your perfect day out as a couple look like? A walk in the park and a movie? A fancy dinner and a night in a smart hotel? Maybe you're not thinking creatively enough. Maybe you need to inject some hospital gowns and ultrasound gel into proceedings ...

Abbey: I'm anxious about my health and my family's health. I suppose everyone is, a bit. But we have more reason to be this way than some.

When Sophia was just a few months old, she needed surgery. It meant being in Great Ormond Street Hospital for three weeks, under the care of a world-famous doctor whose nickname was the Man with the Golden Knife. I'll never forget sitting in that waiting room while the operation was underway. The longest, worst wait of our lives.

And when the doctor called and told us that everything was fine and that our little girl would be OK, I can't begin to describe the relief. I ran into the hospital, jumped on him, wrapped my legs around his waist and full-on nearly snogged him.

Peter: The doctor turned to his trainee and said, 'Just so you know, not every day is like this. Today is a particularly good day.'

Abbey: Ever since then, I've been health-obsessed. I've been blocked by quite a few doctors now, because I always ask for their personal phone numbers and call them in the middle of the night if I'm worried about something. And I'm *always* worried about something.

Peter: It's not just phone calls. It's videos of the babies breathing. *Is this normal?* It's photos of their poo. *IS THIS NORMAL?!!!!* It's not a complete surprise that they don't want to receive that kind of thing at two in the morning.

Abbey: My favourite doctor is a parent at the children's school. He has a lovely, compassionate bedside manner. He listens to all my problems and worries, and he gives me calm, sensible advice. But even he has had to say to me, 'Abbey, nobody's ill except for you, in the head. Maybe you should go and talk to someone about this.'

Peter: But nobody's going to talk Abs out of her health anxiety. If she has a cough, the end is nigh. She's forever calling our doctor to demand a test or a scan or an X-ray. So we've developed a way to make these little paranoias a pleasant part of our everyday lives.

Most people head up to London for a special meal or a

bit of sightseeing. Maybe they'll visit a gallery or take in a show. Not us. For us, a perfect day out comprises a trip to a nice antiseptic hospital for a lovely X-ray or – if we're really pushing the boat out – an MRI. And then: cocktails.

We can think of no finer way to spend a day together. We get into town, we get tested, then we get a spot of lunch. What could be nicer or more romantic than that?

Y

Y is for Yolo

You only live once. A reassuring mantra when you're about to pour yourself another glass of wine, or buy that pair of shoes you've had your eye on. But maybe there's more to Yolo than that ...

Abbey: You only live once is a saying we live our lives by. We're here for a good time, not a long time, and you have to make the most of your days on this earth. I like to think we do a pretty good job of that.

Peter: You've got to enjoy yourself and make time for each other, which means Yolo is a cornerstone of our relationship. We love and live for our kids, but sometimes you have to make an effort to carve out a bit of time just for the two of you. We try to get away now and then, just for a couple of days, to reconnect, because ... Yolo.

Abbey: Yolo has become a family ethos. But it's more than just an excuse to do whatever the hell you want. It's not simply carte blanche for hedonism. Pete and I have a lot of get up and go. We know how fortunate we are to be doing jobs we love. We're not lazy people. We don't lie in. We try to cram into our lives as much as we possibly can. And so Yolo means that we're constantly reminding (they would say nagging) our kids to make as much as possible of the opportunities life offers them. If one of the kids doesn't want to do their tennis lessons and reminds me – quite correctly – that I'm absolutely rubbish at every sport, I tell them, 'That's the whole point. Don't settle for second best. You only live once. Don't let the opportunity pass you by.'

So: Yolo. Enjoy your life. Make the most of what you have. Go to that party. Eat that cake. But also: learn that sport. Pass that exam. And seize the day.

Peter: Because one day that scan isn't going to be followed by a cocktail ...

Y is for ours is Mine, Mine is Mine

Because caring is sharing.

Isn't it?

Peter: Let's make one thing clear. Abbey earns her own money. She's self-sufficient. Or at least she *could* be self-sufficient. But somehow it doesn't quite work out that way. Somehow it works out that what's hers is hers, and what's mine is hers.

Abbey: I'm not proud of it. And sometimes I think it would be nice to have the satisfaction of buying my own things a bit more often. I felt great pride when I bought my first house, but I can't quite bring myself to waste money on a Gucci handbag. Pete can buy that.

Peter: If you say so, Your Majesty.

It's not even just a money thing. It's also a pudding thing. I've lost count of the number of tiramisus I've ordered. I don't even like tiramisu! But it somehow makes Abs feel better if *I* order it and *she* eats it. Because what's hers is hers, and what's mine is hers.

Abbey: It makes me sound like a right bitch. I think we should devote some space to how lovely I am most of the time. I really don't think we've done a deep enough dive into that particular subject.

Peter: Why don't we devote some space to a discussion of what happens when I offer to make you a cup of tea, and you say no, and I make myself one, then we sit together on the couch and you prise the tea from my reluctant hands and chug it?

Abbey: That does happen from time to time. Can't deny it.

Peter: Or if we go to McDonald's, and I offer you a lovely Big Mac and fries. You'll tell me you're not hungry, that you just want a coffee. And I'll make it very clear: this will be my Big Mac. Not *your* Big Mac. *My* Big Mac. All for *me*. But somehow it never seems to end up that way. Somehow I always seem to end up with a meagre portion of fries and not even a bite of burger.

Abbey: It just makes me feel better if I don't order something. The 'yours is mine, mine is mine' mantra isn't limited to bags, brews and burgers, though. I have plenty of pairs of pyjamas, but I'll always put one of Pete's T-shirts on for bed. Surely that's a woman's prerogative. Surely that's fair payment for the amount of Elemis Pro-Collagen Marine Cream he steals from me when his own face-product supplies have run out.

Peter: It's certainly true that while Abbey gets first dibs on tiramisu and Big Macs, I have the best-moisturised face in the family.

Abbey: So at the end of the day, I'm going to say it all balances out.

Z

Z is for zzzzz

Who's worked the hardest? Who's had the most – or the least – sleep? It can be an exhausting business, getting to the bottom of which of you is the tiredest ...

Peter: We don't argue much. But what we do argue about is who is the most tired. They call it competitive tiredness, and nobody's more competitive than us. I'll come home from work and moan about how knackered I am. Abbey will have been busy all day with the children, so she's not exactly well-rested from a lazy day in the hammock. She'll tell me I have absolutely no right to be more tired than her, and before you know it we're bickering like children and the tiredness competition has zoomed through the group stages and into the knockout round.

'I'm *exhausted* ...'

'You think *you're* exhausted? I was up at six and I've been looking after the kids for ten hours.'

To which there is, admittedly, no good answer.

Abbey: There's only one thing more boring than talking about how tired you are. It's talking about how 'golf tired' you are. When it comes to boring tiredness conversation, that one takes the cake. Pete will come home from three days away with friends, during which time he's done nothing but play golf and have fun. He'll have had a little drink at the airport on the way, a little drink all day every day, a little drink all night every night. He'll have gone to bed late and been up at the crack of dawn to swing the nine irons, all of which means he'll have had very little sleep. And boy, does he let me know about it. He comes home half-dead, but if he wants sympathy he's looking in the wrong place. I don't think it's fair that I get Shattered Pete or Hungover Pete when his friends have had the pleasure of Fun Pete's company all weekend.

I'm not alone. After their last trip, one of Pete's friends arrived home and went straight to bed. His wife marched upstairs, pulled off the duvet and dragged him back downstairs. You go, girl!

Peter: He got thrown out of the bedroom for being too tired. It doesn't seem right.

Abbey: Rubbish. When we have one heavy night out, you're always declaring that you'll never drink again as long as you live. But when you're with the lads you can do it for three days in a row without getting grumpy. If you're able to rally yourself for your mates, you're able to rally yourself for your wife. I'd like a bit of Fun Pete's company too.

Peter: You get Fun Pete when we go out together.

Abbey: I either get Too Much Fun Pete or I get Bloody Boring I'm-too-tired Pete. Often one follows the other. Too Much Fun Pete is unstoppable. He's singing, he's dancing, he's playing air guitar. Sometimes I have to head Bloody Boring Pete off at the pass: 'You'll regret this in the morning. Go to bed now. Get some Zs.' I practically have to drag him kicking and screaming to bed.

And when he wakes in the morning, he always thanks me for it: 'Abs, you were right, you absolutely spotted it.' Of course I spotted it! I don't want a day of competitive tiredness, and Too Much Fun Pete is hot to handle.

Peter: I do occasionally get carried away, it's true. It's hard not to. A lot of our friends are younger than us, so they can stay up for hours and drink shots to their 20-something hearts' content. We've learned now to slip away, like ghosts. That way nobody says goodbye, which would mean being forced to stay for another drink.

Abbey: It's hard to slip off sneakily when you're six-foot-seven, but it's worth it if it means grabbing a few more Zzzzzzs and avoiding the most boring conversation a couple can have. *I'm so tired!*

Epilogue

So when all is said and done, what is the secret to a happy ever after?

Abbey: At the end of it all, we have been through a lot together. We've also travelled a long way, both metaphorically and physically, mainly up and down the M62 when transfer day came around. It's been a hell of a journey and one I'd only ever have wanted to do with you by my side. We're still talking to one another, we're still happily married and we still do genuinely love each other, so what is the secret that we'd like to share? What is the one thing that helps us stay the course?

Peter: Aside from the idea that you are always right?

Abbey: OK, what's one other thinq that helps us stay the course?

It's got to be laughter. No one makes me laugh the way Pete does. We cry with laughter. Even when I'm cross with him, he still makes me laugh and I can't help but stop being cross at him. He makes the kids laugh. He makes everyone laugh. And it was the way he made me laugh when I first met him that made me know instinctively that he was the one. We haven't stopped laughing ever since. A family that laughs together, stays together. A couple who find even the silliest things funny will still be laughing together well into their eighties.

I'm looking forward to that.

Acknowledgements

We would like to thank:

Our listeners who have supported our podcast so far. Without you guys there wouldn't even be a book.

Our family, friends and beautiful children who inspire our stories and fill our lives with so much love, fun and happiness.

R John and R Ross who bring our vision, however ridiculous, to life.

Our publishers at Penguin, especially Charlotte who has been so patient and had so much faith in us.

And Adam for penning the way and saving the day.

Abbey Clancy is a model, television presenter and podcaster. She was the runner-up of *Britain's Next Top Model* in 2006, winner of *Strictly Come Dancing* in 2013 and went on to present *Britain's Next Top Model*. Later this year she will host *Celebrity Homes* on ITV.

Peter Crouch was a professional footballer for over 20 years. He scored over 100 Premier League goals, has 42 England caps and holds the record for the most headed goals in Premier League history. He's now a bestselling author, award-winning podcast host and champion of grassroots football.

Together they host *The Therapy Crouch* podcast, for more information or to follow Abbey and Peter online:

SUNDAY TIMES BESTSELLER
'GENIUS'
DAILY MAIL
'NATIONAL TREASURE'
DAILY TELEGRAPH
I,ROBOT
HOW TO BE A
FOOTBALLER 2
PETER
CROUCH
'ONE OF THE
FUNNIEST HUMAN
BEINGS ON THE
PLANET'
ROMESH RANGANATHAN
'PETER CROUCH
SCORES AGAIN'
THE TIMES MAGAZINE

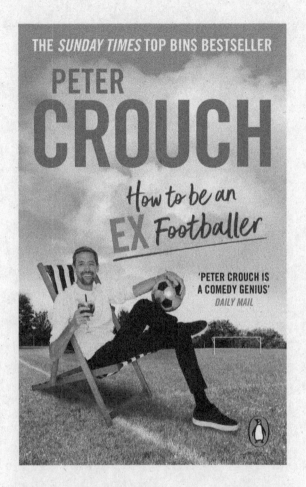